SIGNING EVERYDAY PHRASES

MICKEY FLODIN

A PERIGEE BOOK

A PERIGEE BOOK
Published by the Penguin Group
Penguin Group (USA) Inc.
375 Hudson Street, New York, New York 10014, USA
Penguin Group (Canada), 90 Eglinton Avenue East, Suite 700, Toronto, Ontario M4P 2Y3, Canada
(a division of Pearson Penguin Canada Inc.)
Penguin Books Ltd., 80 Strand, London WC2R 0RL, England
Penguin Group Ireland, 25 St. Stephen's Green, Dublin 2, Ireland (a division of Penguin Books Ltd.)
Penguin Group (Australia), 250 Camberwell Road, Camberwell, Victoria 3124, Australia
(a division of Pearson Australia Group Pty. Ltd.)
Penguin Books India Pvt. Ltd., 11 Community Centre, Panchsheel Park, New Delhi—110 017, India
Penguin Group (NZ), 67 Apollo Drive, Rosedale, North Shore 0745, Auckland, New Zealand
(a division of Pearson New Zealand Ltd.)
Penguin Books (South Africa) (Pty.) Ltd., 24 Sturdee Avenue, Rosebank, Johannesburg 2196,
South Africa

Penguin Books Ltd., Registered Offices: 80 Strand, London WC2R 0RL, England

While the author has made every effort to provide accurate telephone numbers and Internet addresses at the time of publication, neither the publisher nor the author assumes any responsibility for errors, or for changes that occur after publication. Further, the publisher does not have any control over and does not assume any responsibility for author or third-party websites or their content.

First Perigee edition: October 1996

Library of Congress Cataloging-in-Publication Data

Flodin, Mickey.
  Signing everyday phrases / Mickey Flodin.—1st ed.
    p. cm.
  "A Perigee book."
  Includes index.
  ISBN 978-0-399-52236-9
1. American Sign Language—Terms and phrases. I. Title.
HV2474.F55   1996
419—dc20   96-23260   CIP

PRINTED IN THE UNITED STATES OF AMERICA

30   29   28   27   26   25   24   23   22   21

Most Perigee Books are available at special quantity discounts for bulk purchases for sales promotions, premiums, fund-raising, or educational use. Special books, or book excerpts, can also be created to fit specific needs. For details, write: Special Markets, Penguin Group (USA) Inc., 375 Hudson Street, New York, New York 10014.

CONTENTS

ACKNOWLEDGMENTS

My sincere thanks to several individuals who helped make this book possible.

Carol Flodin, my companion and best friend, who generously gave of her time to proof the final text, compile and check the index, and offer many invaluable suggestions.

Daniel Flodin, my son, who helped assemble the book on computer.

John Duff, publisher, Perigee Books, for his support for this project.

Karen Twigg, for reviewing the text, and for her suggestions. Karen has been a sign language teacher and interpreter for over 27 years. At Akron University, she studied interpreting skills and later taught at B.B.C., Springfield, MO. Her B.A. and M.S. in education were earned at Southwest Missouri University, Springfield, MO. Karen has used her exceptional interpreting skills in hospitals, schools, courtrooms, and churches, and has taught interpreter's classes, as well.

INTRODUCTION

T here is no doubt that signing is popular. We see people signing everywhere—at school, on television, in movies, in stores, at home—anywhere people are. And why not? Signing is expressive and rewarding to learn. Most of all, American Sign Language (ASL) is the native language of the Deaf community in the U.S. It is a visual-gesture language that was developed over many years by deaf people to communicate with each other. It has a different syntax and grammatical rules than English and is preferred by deaf people when communicating among themselves.

When hearing and deaf people sign together, they usually take the signs of ASL and put them in English word order. This is easier for hearing people. This is known as Signed English (SE). SE also incorporates the body language and facial expressions of ASL. Although signs were originally created to represent concepts and not words, SE is an acceptable method of communication. This signing system is combined with speech and fingerspelling and is known as simultaneous communication.

ABOUT THIS BOOK

S *igning Everyday Phrases* has been written to give hospital workers, doctors, police, firefighters, emergency personnel, social and government workers, scouting personnel, waiters and waitresses—anyone who comes in contact with deaf people—a basic sign language vocabulary to express common, everyday ideas, events, and feelings. Many people in the workplace have patients, clients, customers, or friends who are deaf. Communication is essential, and learning to sign makes better communication possible. Wouldn't you like to know how to "talk" with your hands? Well, now you can. *Signing Everyday Phrases* will guide you step-by-step. You'll be signing in only a short time. This book will prove to be invaluable to family members and friends, as well, for it contains many of the sentences commonly used in everyday life.

Signing Everyday Phrases is exactly that. The phrases and sentences you probably use every day are illustrated here in sign language. Since most, if not all, of the sentences are already familiar in their English form, signing them will be that much easier. *Signing Everyday Phrases* contains the basic signs in use in the United States and Canada, though there may be some local variations.

This book has 13 categorized chapters, each containing many sentences related to one or more similar subjects. The sentences were written to stand alone and do not collectively tell a story. Many sentences contain one or two words in parentheses (). These words can be used in place of the previous word or phrase. Example: *Good morning (night)* can be signed *Good morning* or *Good night*. Also, the last page or two of each chapter (except chapters 1 and 2) has a short sentence with several replacement signs to choose from. This gives the student several possible sentences to sign. Even so, don't be afraid to be creative. If a needed sentence can't be found, combine two sentences or change a question to a statement. Also there are many synonyms to choose from in the index.

As you begin, learn the manual alphabet first, for it will expand your ability to communicate. Also, many signs have "initialized" hand shapes (more on this later). If you prefer, you can skip from chapter to chapter picking out the sentences or signs you wish or need to learn, or simply start at the beginning of the book.

Look at the illustration(s) and arrow(s) for the correct hand shape and movement of the sign. Then read the description. Sometimes the sign is repeated, or the hands may "alternate," or they may "move simultaneously."

The Dominant Hand
Some signs are performed using two different hand shapes. The dominant hand provides the movement while the other hand is motionless. An example is *sing*.

Sing

All the signs are illustrated for a right-handed person. Some left-handed people may feel it is impossible to use the right hand as the dominant hand, but making the signs with the left hand reverses the signs to the receiver. If possible, use the right hand.

Sign Directions
Most of the signs in this book show the sign as you would see someone signing to you. However, a number of signs are shown from an angle or profile perspective or close up to make the signs clearer and easier to follow. Remember to face the person you are signing with.

A FEW BASICS

The Manual Alphabet and Fingerspelling

Fingerspelling is used to spell out words one letter at a
time with the manual alphabet. It is important to learn to
fingerspell to communicate with deaf people. Fingerspelling
is used for names of people, places, and words for which
there are no signs, or as a substitute when the sign has not
been learned. Memorize the manual alphabet at the beginning of learning sign language. Many of the manual alphabet hand shapes are easy to remember because they
resemble the configuration of English letters. The entire
manual alphabet can be memorized in a short time. Then
start fingerspelling two- and three-letter words before
moving on to larger words.

Fingerspelling
Position

When fingerspelling, hold your hand in a comfortable
position near the shoulder, with the palm facing forward.
Don't make exaggerated hand or arm movements. Combine
the letters smoothly and at a comfortable rate. Pause slightly at the end of each word but do not drop the hands
between words. It is important to speak or mouth the
word, not the letter, as you begin to fingerspell it.

Words with double letters (*keep*) can be fingerspelled
by opening the hand slightly between letters. For words
with double open letters, such as *will*, move the *L* hand to
the right with a small bounce to sign the second letter *L*.

When receiving or reading fingerspelling, learn to read
words in syllables or entire words, rather than individual
letters. This may be difficult at first but it will help you
grasp the word more quickly.

The Signing Area

Most signs are made within an imaginary rectangle in front
of the body—an area extending from the top of the head to
the waist, and just beyond the shoulders. This allows the
eyes to follow the sign's movement more readily and makes
the signs easier to understand. Pause when you are in
between thoughts or sentences, or waiting for a response,
by holding your hand in a comfortable position at chest
level or at your side.

The Signing
Area

Pronouns

In sign language, pronouns can be indicated by pointing to
an imaginary spot or location. Each time you mention a

particular person, point to them, if present, or to their imaginary location. Several people can be discussed at the same time by pointing to their respective spots or locations.

Understanding Present, Past, and Future Time
It is important to understand the sign language concept of present, past, and future time. Think of the area immediately in front of the body as representing *present* time. Therefore, signs dealing with present time are made in front of the body, such as *now*. Signs referring to the future, such as *tomorrow*, have a forward movement away from the body. Signs that deal with the past, such as *last year*, move backward from the present time reference place.

Signing Capitals
When capitals or abbreviations are fingerspelled, such as *U.S.A.*, they need to be differentiated from other letters or words. This is done by circling (to the right) each letter slightly as you sign it.

How to Use the *Person-Ending* Sign

Person Ending

The *person-ending* sign usually relates to a person's occupation, position in life, or nationality and is always used after another sign. It is made by holding both flat open hands to the front with palms facing; then move them down simultaneously. Some examples: sign *photograph* plus the *person ending* for *photographer*; sign *airplane* plus the *person ending* for *pilot*.

Possessives and Plurals
For the purposes of this book, possessives (*'s*) and plurals are generally understood within context. However, they may be needed for teaching deaf students English. If you decide to use them, see page 12.

Questions and Punctuation
Punctuation marks, such as the period and question mark, are not usually used in signing. A quizzical or questioning facial expression and body language or the context will help convey that you are asking a question. To indicate the end of a thought or sentence, just pause for a moment. If you need to use punctuation, see page 12.

Definite and Indefinite Articles
Definite and indefinite articles (*a, an,* and *the*) are often

used by hearing people when signing, especially to teach deaf students English, but some people may prefer not to sign them. Therefore, the signs for articles are shown in the sentences where they occur, but signing them is optional.

Numbers, Money, and Years

Money amounts, years, addresses, and telephone numbers are signed as they are spoken in English. To express the amount $19.42, sign *nineteen (19) dollars four two (4 2) cents.* For the year 1996, sign *nineteen (19) nine six (9 6).* The address 735 Lake Shore Drive is signed *7 3 5 Lake Shore Drive* (the words are signed and/or fingerspelled). The digits of a telephone number are signed as they are spoken; the number 555-3674, for example, is signed *5 5 5* (pause) *3 6 7 4.*

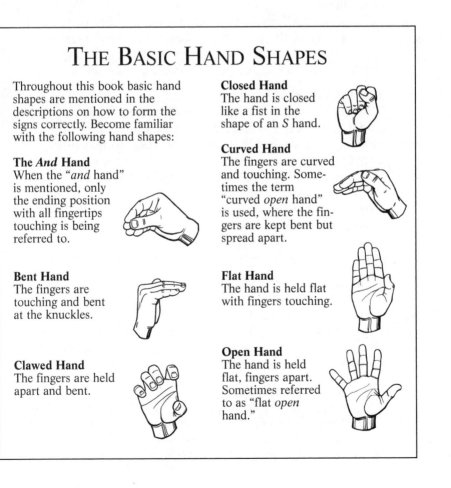

THE BASIC HAND SHAPES

Throughout this book basic hand shapes are mentioned in the descriptions on how to form the signs correctly. Become familiar with the following hand shapes:

The *And* Hand

When the "*and* hand" is mentioned, only the ending position with all fingertips touching is being referred to.

Bent Hand

The fingers are touching and bent at the knuckles.

Clawed Hand

The fingers are held apart and bent.

Closed Hand

The hand is closed like a fist in the shape of an *S* hand.

Curved Hand

The fingers are curved and touching. Sometimes the term "curved *open* hand" is used, where the fingers are kept bent but spread apart.

Flat Hand

The hand is held flat with fingers touching.

Open Hand

The hand is held flat, fingers apart. Sometimes referred to as "flat *open* hand."

Tips for Better Signing

Initialized Signs
As you begin to learn signing, you will notice that a number of signs are "initialized." The term refers to a sign formed with the fingerspelled hand shape of the first letter of the English word. Two examples are *aunt,* made with an *A* hand, and *education*, made with *E* hands.

Uncle

The Locations of Gender Signs
The male and female gender signs are identified more easily by their locations. Many male-related signs are made near the forehead, while many female-related signs are made near the cheek or chin (see *uncle* and *aunt* at left).

Aunt

Opposites
You will soon discover that there are a number of pairs of signs that have the same hand shape, but have a reverse movement and, quite often, are opposite in meaning. Two examples are: *come* and *go*; and *open* and *close*.

The Symmetry of Signs
Whenever a sign requires both hands to move or to be active, both hands will have the same hand shape although there are a few signs that do not conform to this rule. Conversely, when both hands have a different hand shape, only the dominant hand moves. This principle also holds true for the motion of the sign as well. When both hands move—in any direction—the type of motion, even if alternating, will be the same for both hands. Example: The sign for *family* has two *F* hands, and the motion or movement of each hand is the same.

Imagination

Thinking and Feeling Signs
Signs that deal with thinking or mental activity are usually made at or near the head. An example is *imagination*. Another group of signs are those that deal with *feelings*. Many of these signs are done in the chest area near or at the heart, such as *happy*.

Now You Are Ready
You are beginning a rewarding and fascinating journey into signing and will soon discover (if you haven't already) the thrill and satisfaction of "talking" with your hands. Welcome to *Signing Everyday Phrases.*

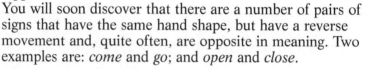

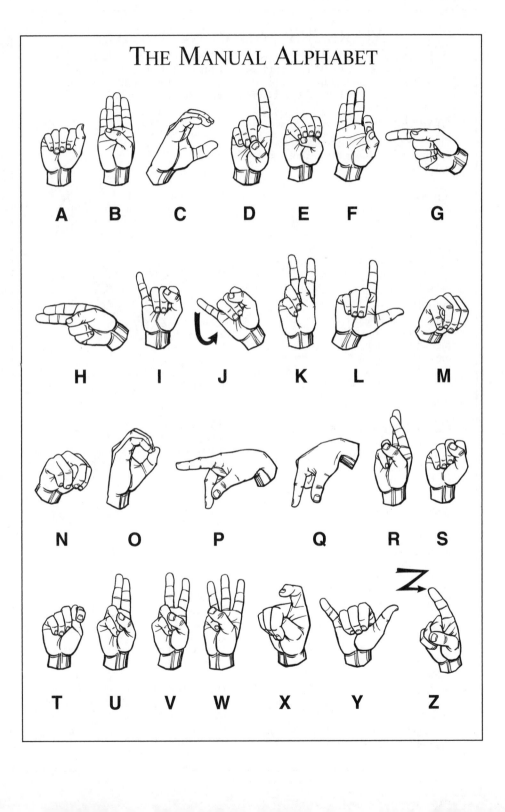

The Manual Alphabet

A B C D E F G

H I J K L M

N O P Q R S

T U V W X Y Z

MARKERS AND PUNCTUATION

The following markers (inflections or word endings) and punctuation are used as "teaching tools" to teach deaf students English. They are not needed to sign the sentences in this book. If they are used, it is recommended that the basic signs be learned first before these are added to them.

MARKERS

They are added after a basic sign (or fingerspelled word) to express a word exactly.

-MENT

Place the modified *M* hand near the top of the flat left hand; then move the modified *M* hand down to the base of the left hand.

-NESS

Place the modified *N* hand near the top of the flat left hand and move the modified *N* hand down to the base of the left hand.

-ER (Comparative Degree)

Face both *A* hands in front, right *A* hand lower, and move the right *A* hand up slightly above the left hand.

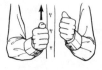

-EST (Superlative Degree)

Place both *A* hands in front, facing each other, with right hand lower than left, and move the right *A* hand high above the left.

-ING

The *I* hand faces left, then twist it to the right.

-'S or S' (possessives)

The *S* hand faces left, then twist it to the right.

-S
S hand.

-ED

Sign *past* by moving the right upraised flat hand backward over the right shoulder with palm facing the body.

-ED (*alternative*)
D hand.

-EN
N hand.

-Y
Y hand.

-LY

Sign "I love you" hand shape and move downward in a wavy movement.

-LY (*alternative*)
Sign *L*; then sign *Y*.

PUNCTUATION MARKS

PERIOD, QUESTION, APOSTROPHE, COLON, COMMA, EXCLAMATION POINT, SEMICOLON

Draw the shape of the appropriate punctuation mark in the air with the right index finger or with the right index finger and thumb touching, other fingers closed.

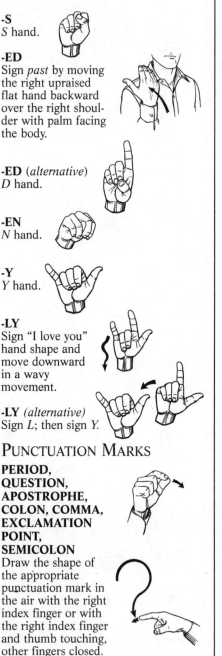

Greetings and Introductions

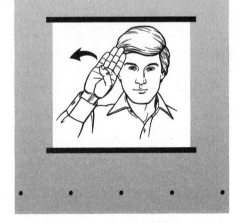

 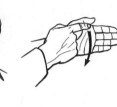 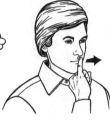 

Hi.   What   is   your

name?   My   name   is

 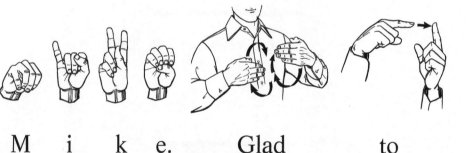

M   i   k   e.   Glad   to

GLAD, HAPPY, JOY: Move the flat hands in forward circles as fingers touch the chest alternately or in unison. One hand can be used.
HI, HELLO: Place the right *B* hand at the forehead and move it to the right. Or fingerspell *H–I.*
IS: Place right *I* hand at the mouth and move it forward.
MY, MINE, OWN: Place the right flat hand on the chest.
NAME: Cross both *H* fingers.

TO: Touch the left vertical index fingertip with the right index fingertip.
WHAT: Move the tip of the right index finger across the left flat palm.
YOUR, YOURS, HIS, HER, THEIR: Push the right flat palm forward toward the person being spoken to. If it is not clear from the context, the *male* or *female* sign can be used first. When using *your* in the plural, push the right flat palm forward, then

move it to the right.

  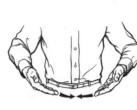 

meet   you.   Introduce   your

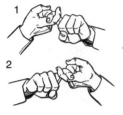   

friend.   This   is   K i m.

   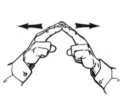

How   are   you?   Very

ARE: Move the right *R* hand forward from the lips.

FRIEND, FRIENDSHIP: Hook the right index finger over the left index finger, then reverse the movement.

HOW: Place both bent hands together back to back. Turn them forward until both hands are flat with palms up.

INTRODUCE: Place the flat hands at the sides and move them to the center until fingertips almost touch.

IS: Place the right *I* hand at the mouth and move it forward.

MEET, ENCOUNTER: Extend the index fingers of both hands and hold them at the sides with palms facing.

THIS: Place the right index in the left flat palm for something specific.

VERY: Place both *V*-hand fingertips together and move them apart.

YOU: Point to the person

you are signing to. Move the right hand from left to right if there is more than one person.

YOUR, YOURS, HIS, HER, THEIR: Push the right flat palm forward toward the person being spoken to. If it is not clear from the context, the *male* or *female* sign can be used first. When using *your* in the plural, push the right flat palm forward, then move it to the right.

good.   Fine.   Where   are

you   from?   Have   we

   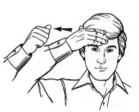

met   before?   I   forgot

ARE: *(See page 15.)*
BEFORE (time): Hold both slightly curved hands to the front near each other, right behind left. Move the right hand backward.
FINE: Hold thumb of right open flat hand on chest and move it up and forward.
FORGOT, FORGET, FOR-SAKE: Move the right open hand, palm in, across the forehead from left to right, ending with the *A* hand to the right of the head.

FROM: Touch the right *X* index finger on the left vertical index finger and move it back and away.
GOOD, WELL: Touch the lips with the right flat hand. Then bring the right hand down into the left hand with both palms up.
HAVE, HAD, HAS, OWN, POSSESS: Move the bent hands, placing the fingertips on the chest.
I: Place the right *I* hand on chest with palm facing left.

MET, MEET, ENCOUNTER: Extend index fingers of both hands and hold them at the sides with palms facing. Bring both hands together.
WE, US: Touch the right shoulder with the right index finger. Then, circle it forward and back until it touches the left shoulder. The *W* can be used for *we* and *U* for *us*.
WHERE: Shake the right index finger back and forth.
YOU: *(See page 15.)*

your name. Please repeat.

Good morning (afternoon) (night).

You're welcome. It is nice

AFTERNOON: Hold the right forearm at a 45-degree angle on the back of the left flat hand, which is horizontal and palm down.

GOOD, WELL: Touch the lips with the right flat hand. Then bring the right hand down into the left hand with both palms up.

IS: Place the right *I* hand at the mouth and move it forward.

IT: Touch the right *I* finger in the flat left palm.

MORNING: Bend the left arm and rest the left hand in the bend of the right arm. Hold the right hand flat and arm bent horizontally. Move the right arm upright, palm facing self.

NAME: Cross both *H* fingers.

NICE, CLEAN, PURE: Pass the right flat hand over the palm of the left hand.

NIGHT, EVENING: Place the right curved hand over the flat horizontal left hand.

PLEASE, ENJOY, LIKE, PLEASURE: Put the right hand over the heart. Move the hand in a small circle.

REPEAT, AGAIN: Turn the bent right hand up and into the flat left palm.

YOU'RE WELCOME, THANKS, THANK YOU: Smile and bring the fingertips of both flat hands to the lips. Move the hands forward until palms are up. The right hand can be used.

YOUR: *(See page 15.)*

 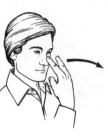  

to   see   you.   Come

 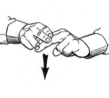  

in.   Sit   please.   Sorry,

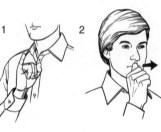 

I'm   late.   Sign

AM: Move the right *A*-hand thumb forward from the lips.
COME: Circle the index fingers as they move toward the body.
I: Place the right *I* hand on the chest with the palm facing left.
IN: Place the right *and*-hand fingertips into the left *C* hand.
LATE, NOT YET: Move the right flat hand back and forth a few times near the right side.

PLEASE, ENJOY, LIKE, PLEASURE: Put the right hand over the heart. Move the hand in a small circle.
SEE, SIGHT, VISION: Point the right *V* fingertips toward the eyes. Then move the hand forward.
SIGN (language): Point the index fingers toward each other, palms out, and rotate them in alternating backward circles.
SIT, BE SEATED, SEAT: Hold the right *H* fingers on

the left *H* fingers and push both hands down a little.
SORRY, APOLOGY, REGRET, SORROW: Make a circle over the heart with the right *A* (or *S*) hand.
TO: Touch the left vertical index fingertip with the right index fingertip.
YOU: Point to the person you are signing to. Move the right hand from left to right if there is more than one person.

slowly.

Excuse

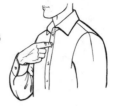
me.

Do

you

have

time

for

tea

or

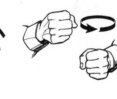
coffee?

Yes.

COFFEE: Hold both *S* hands forward and move the right hand in a circle over the left.

DO, ACTION, DID, DONE: Move both downturned *C* hands in unison to the left, then to the right.

EXCUSE, FORGIVE, PARDON: Move right fingertips over the lower part of the left flat hand a few times.

FOR: Place the right index finger at the right temple. Twist it forward as the hand moves forward.

HAVE, HAD, HAS, OWN, POSSESS: Move the bent hands, placing the fingertips on the chest.

ME: Point to or touch the chest with the right index finger.

OR, EITHER: Touch the left *L*-hand thumb and index finger several times with the right index finger.

SLOW: Slide the right hand slowly over back of left hand from fingertips to wrist.

TEA: Circle the thumb and index of the right *F* hand above the left *O* hand.

TIME, CLOCK, WATCH: Tap the left wrist a few times with the right curved index finger.

YES: Move the right *S* hand up and down.

YOU: Point to the person you are signing to. Move the right hand from left to right if there is more than one person.

  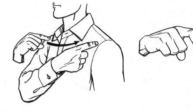

No.　　Thank you.　　We　　need

to　　leave　　now　　(soon).

Are　　you　　ready　　to

ARE: Move the right *R* hand forward from the lips.
LEAVE, DEPART, RETIRE: Hold flat hands to the right, palms down. Draw them up to self, ending in *A* hands.
NEED, HAVE TO, MUST, NECESSARY, SHOULD: Move the right bent index finger down forcefully several times.
NO: Touch right middle and index fingers with thumb.
NOW, CURRENT, IMMEDI-ATE: Quickly drop both bent

(or *Y*) hands in front of the body at the waist, palms up.
READY, ORDER, PLAN: Hold both flat hands a little to the left, palms facing. Move them together to the right in small up-and-down movements. *R* hands can be used for *ready* and *P* hands for *plan*.
SOON, BRIEF, SHORT (length or time): Cross *H* hands and slide, back and forth, right fingers over left.
THANK YOU, THANKS,

YOU'RE WELCOME: Smile and hold flat hands to the lips. Move the hands forward until palms are up. The right hand can be used.
TO: Touch the left vertical index fingertip with the right index fingertip.
WE, US: Touch the right shoulder with the right index finger. Then, circle it forward and back until it touches the left shoulder. The *W* can be used for *we* and *U* for *us*.
YOU: *(See page 19.)*

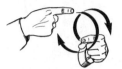   

go?   Almost.   Please   hold

this.   When   can   you

visit?   Kiss   grandmother   (grandfather).

ALMOST, NEARLY: With both palms up, move the little-finger edge of the right hand up, hitting the fingertips of the left curved hand.

CAN, ABILITY, ABLE, COMPETENT, COULD, POSSIBLE: Move both *S* (or *A*) hands down together.

GO: Circle the index fingers around each other as they move forward.

GRANDFATHER: Touch the thumb of the right open hand on the forehead. Move

it forward in two small arcs.

GRANDMOTHER: Touch the chin with the thumb of the right open hand. Move it forward in two small arcs.

HOLD: Place the *S* hands in front of the body, with right hand over left hand, palms in, and move them toward the body.

KISS: Touch the right hand fingers on the lips, then on the right cheek.

PLEASE, ENJOY, LIKE, PLEASURE: Put the right

hand over the heart and move it in a small circle.

THIS: Place the right index finger in the left flat palm for something specific.

VISIT: Place both *V* hands up, palms in. Move them in alternating forward circles.

WHEN: Move the right index finger around the left upright index finger. Then touch the tip of the right index finger on the tip of the left index finger.

YOU: *(See page 19.)*

I will write. Call
telephone

me on the T T Y*.

   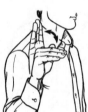

See you later. Good-bye.

CALL, TELEPHONE: Hold the thumb of the right *Y* hand to the ear.

GOOD-BYE: Bend the right flat hand up and down.

I: Place the right *I* hand on the chest with the palm facing left.

LATER, AFTER, AFTER A WHILE: Hold the right *L* hand in the vertical left palm and twist it forward and down.

ME: Point to or touch the chest with the right index finger.

ON: Place the right flat hand on the top of the left flat hand, palms down.

SEE, SIGHT, VISION: Point the right *V* fingertips toward the eyes. Then move the hand forward.

THE (definite article): Twist the right *T* hand to the right from a palm-left position.

WILL (verb), SHALL, WOULD: Hold the flat right hand to the right side of the face and move it forward.

WRITE: Pretend to be writing on the left flat palm with the right index finger and thumb.

YOU: Point to the person you are signing to. Move the hand from left to right if there is more than one person.

*Teletypewriters are telecommunications devices for deaf people.

Home, Family, and Friends

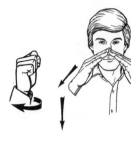 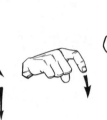 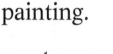  

The   house   needs   painting.

   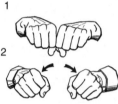

This   glass   is   broken.
substance

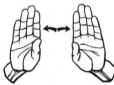 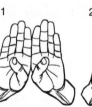 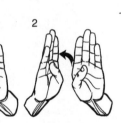 

Open   the   door.   Turn

BROKEN, BREAK, FRAC-TURE, SNAP: Place the *S* hands to the front and touching. Twist them quickly down and apart like *break-ing* a branch.

DOOR: Place the *B* hands to the front, palms out, and side-by-side. Turn the right hand back and forth.

GLASS (substance), DISH: Touch the front teeth with the curved right index finger.

HOUSE: Outline the shape of a house with the flat hands.

IS: Place the right *I* hand at the mouth and move it forward.

NEED, HAVE TO, MUST, NECESSARY, SHOULD: Move the right bent index finger down forcefully several times.

OPEN: Hold both flat-hand palms forward with index finger and thumbs touching. Move hands apart.

PAINT: Slide the right hand fingertips back and forth

over the left palm and fingers.

THE (definite article): Twist the right *T* hand to the right from a palm-left position.

THIS: Place the right index finger in the left flat palm for something specific.

TURN: Rotate the index fingers in right-to-left circles around each other with the right pointing down and left pointing up.

on   the air conditioner (radio)

 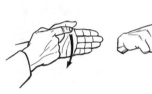   

(TV).   What   should   we

watch?   Videotape   the   movie.

AIR CONDITIONING: Fingerspell *A* then *C*.
MOVIE: Face the palm of the left open hand almost forward. Place the right open hand on the left hand and move the right hand back and forth.
ON: Place the right flat hand on top of the left flat hand, palms down.
RADIO: Place the cupped hands over the ears.
SHOULD, NEED, HAVE TO, MUST, NECESSARY: Move

the right bent index finger down forcefully several times.
TELEVISION: Fingerspell *T* then *V* with the right hand.
THE: *(See page 24.)*
VIDEOTAPE: Rotate the thumb side of the right *V* hand in a circle on the left flat palm, which is facing right. Make the same movement with the right *T* hand on the left flat palm.
WATCH, LOOK, LOOK AT, LOOK AT ME, LOOK BACK, LOOK DOWN, OBSERVE:

Point the right *V* hand to the eyes. Twist the *V* hand and point it forward. For *look at me, look back,* and *look down,* point the *V* hand at the eyes, then in the direction needed.
WE, US: Touch the right shoulder with the right index finger. Then, circle it forward and back until it touches the left shoulder. The *W* can be used for *we* and *U* for *us*.
WHAT: Move tip of right index across left flat palm.

Take   a   shower   (bath).

Wash   the   dirty   clothes.

Brush your teeth.   Go   to   bed.

A: Move the right *A* hand in a small arc to the right.
BATH, BATHE: Rub the *A* hands up and down on the chest a few times.
BED: Put both flat hands together and place them at the right cheek.
BRUSH YOUR TEETH, TOOTHBRUSH: Move the horizontal right index finger up and down in front of the teeth.
CLOTHES, DRESS, SUIT, WEAR: Place the fingertips of the open hands on the chest. Then move them down and repeat.
DIRTY, FILTHY: Wiggle the fingers as the right open hand is held palm down under the chin.
GO: Circle the index fingers around each other as they move forward.
SHOWER: Move the right *and* (or *S*) hand quickly down toward the head, ending with the open hand.
TAKE: Move the right open hand from right to left, ending with a closed hand near the body.
THE (definite article): Twist the right *T* hand to the right from a palm left position.
TO: Touch the left vertical index fingertip with the right index fingertip.
WASH: Rub the *A* hands together in circular motions.

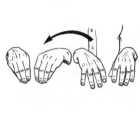   

  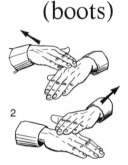

Put	pajamas	(boots)

on.	Wash	your	hands

(face).	Shampoo	your	hair.

BOOTS: Hit the closed hands together several times. Hold the right flat hand in the bend of left arm.
FACE: Circle the face with the right index finger.
HAIR: Hold a lock of hair with the right thumb and index fingers.
HANDS: Slide the right flat hand toward self over the back of the left hand. Reverse hands and repeat the same movement.
ON: Place the right flat hand on top of the left flat hand, palms down.
PAJAMAS: Sign *sleep* and *clothes.* Move the right open hand down the face, ending with the *and* hand at the chin. Next, using flat open hands, move the fingertips down the chest several times.
PUT, MOVE: Hold the open curved hands to the left front, palms down. Move them together up and down to the right while closing them to *and* hands.

SHAMPOO: Form *A* hands with both hands and rub them on sides of the head.
WASH: Rub the *A* hands together in circular motions.
YOUR, YOURS, HIS, HER, THEIR: Push the right flat palm forward toward the person being spoken to. If it is not clear from the context, the *male* or *female* sign can be used first. When using *your* in the plural, push the right flat palm forward, then move it to the right.

  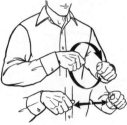

Hang up   the   clothes.   Tie

your   shoes.   Dust   the

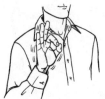  

furniture.   Put   soap   in

CLOTHES, DRESS, SUIT, WEAR: Place the fingertips of the open hands on the chest. Then move them down and repeat.
DUST: The right *A* hand, facing left with palm down, sweeps across the front of the body in a wavy motion.
FURNITURE: Shake right *F* hand back and forth near the right shoulder or in front of chest.
HANG UP, HANGER: Hold the right *X* hand up with palm facing forward. Move it forward and up a little.
IN: Place the right *and*-hand fingertips into left *C* hand.
PUT, MOVE: Hold the open curved hands to the left front, palms down. Move them together up and down to the right while closing them to *and* hands.
SHOES: Tap the *S* hands together a couple of times.
SOAP: Rub the right fingertips across left flat palm a few times.
TIE (a knot): Rotate both modified *A* hands (thumbs in crooks of index fingers) around each other in forward circles. Place hands side by side and pull them apart.
YOUR, YOURS, HIS, HER, THEIR: Push the right flat palm forward toward the person being spoken to. If it is not clear from the context, the *male* or *female* sign can be used first. When using *your* in the plural, push right flat palm forward, then to the right.

  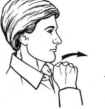 

the washing machine.   Don't   run

(be   stubborn).   Wait   patiently.

Obey   me.   Don't   complain

BE: Place the right *B* hand at the mouth and move it forward.

COMPLAIN, OBJECT, PROTEST: Hit the fingertips of the curved right hand on the chest several times.

DON'T, DOESN'T, DO NOT, NOT: Put the right *A*-hand thumb under the chin. Move it quickly forward.

ME: Point to or touch the chest with the right index finger.

OBEY: Place the *A* hands on the forehead. Then move them down to the front with flat hands turned palms up.

PATIENT, PATIENCE: Slide the right *A* thumb down across the lips.

RUN: Place both flat hands together palm to palm with left hand on top. Then quickly move the right hand forward.

STUBBORN, DONKEY, MULE: Hold the right flat hand at the right side of the head and bend the fingers forward. Two hands can be used.

THE (definite article): Twist the right *T* hand to the right from a palm left position.

WAIT, PENDING: Face both curved open hands to the left, palms up, right behind left, and wiggle the fingers.

WASHING MACHINE: Twist (or rotate) the open curved hands, right over left, in opposite directions.

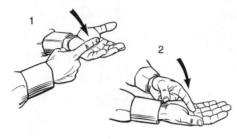

(argue).   My   aunt

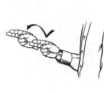

(uncle)   is   hard-of-hearing.   We

are   cousins.   What   should

ARE: Move the right *R* hand forward from the lips.
ARGUE, CONTROVERSY, DEBATE: First strike the left palm with the right index finger and then the right palm with the left index finger. Repeat several times.
AUNT: Shake the right *A* hand near the right cheek.
COUSIN: Shake the right *C* hand near the right temple for a male or near the right cheek (or jaw) for a female.
HARD-OF-HEARING: With

right *H* hand pointing forward, move it to the right in a small arc.
IS: Place the right *I* hand at the mouth and move it forward.
MY, MINE, OWN: Place the right flat hand on the chest.
SHOULD, NEED, HAVE TO, MUST, NECESSARY: Move the right bent index finger down forcefully several times.
UNCLE: Shake the right *U* hand, palm forward, near

the right temple.
WE, US: Touch the right shoulder with the right index finger. Then, circle it forward and back until it touches the left shoulder. The *W* can be used for *we* and *U* for *us*.
WHAT: Move the tip of the right index finger across the left flat palm.

I	wear	to	the

wedding?	How	old	are

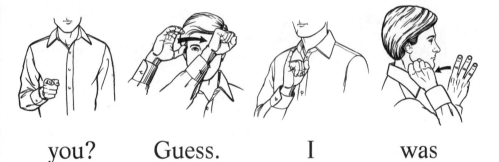

you?	Guess.	I	was

ARE: Move the right *R* hand forward from the lips.

GUESS, MISS (let slip or let go): Move the right *C* hand across the front of the forehead, ending with an *S* hand.

HOW: Place both bent hands together back to back. Turn them forward until the hands are flat, palms up.

I: Place the right *I* hand on the chest, palm left.

OLD, AGE, ANTIQUE: Pretend to be grabbing a beard. Then move the right hand down from under the chin, ending with an *S* hand.

THE (definite article): Twist the right *T* hand to the right from a palm left position.

TO: Touch the left vertical index fingertip with the right index fingertip.

WAS: Move the right *W* hand backward near the right cheek and close it to an *S* hand.

WEAR, CLOTHES, DRESS, SUIT: Place the fingertips of the open hands on the chest. Then move them down and repeat.

WEDDING: Swing the flat hands toward each other in front of the body, ending with the left hand holding the right fingers.

YOU: Point to the person you are signing to. Move the right hand from left to right for more than one person.

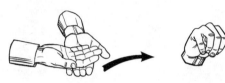

born   M   a   y   15,

19   5   4.   I   need   to

shave.   Get   a   haircut.

A: Move the right *A* hand in a small arc to the right.
BORN, BIRTH: With palms up, hold the right hand in the left hand and move them forward and up.
FIFTEEN: Hold up the right *5* hand, palm facing self, and move all four fingers up and down a few times.
GET: Move the open hands together in front of the body with the right hand on top of the left, forming *S* hands.
HAIRCUT: Place right *H* fin-

gers near the hair and open and close them a few times.
I: Place the right *I* hand on the chest, palm left.
NEED, HAVE TO, MUST, NECESSARY, SHOULD: Move the right bent index finger down forcefully several times.
NINETEEN-FIFTY-FOUR: Sign *nineteen* by holding up the right *A* hand, palm left and thumb extended, then quickly twist the wrist forward while changing to a *9*

hand (touching the tips of the thumb and index finger). Next, sign *five* by holding up the right open hand, palm forward. Then, sign *four* by holding up the separated right four fingers with thumb bent over palm, palm facing forward.
SHAVE: Slide the thumb of the right *Y* hand down the right cheek several times.
TO: Touch the left vertical index fingertip with the right index fingertip.

| Stop | pushing | and | hitting |

 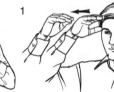 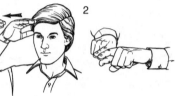

| your | younger | brother. |

| Arrange | your | room. |

AND: Move the right open hand to the right as the hand closes to all fingertips touching.

ARRANGE, ORDER, PLAN, PREPARE, READY: Hold both flat hands a little to the left, palms facing. Move them together to the right in small up and down movements. *R* hands can be used for *ready* and *P* hands for *plan*.

BROTHER: Pretend to be gripping a cap with the right hand. Move hand forward a little. Next place the index fingers together.

HIT: Strike the left index finger, palm up, with the right fist.

PUSH: Push both flat hands forward.

ROOM: With palms facing, hold the flat hands to the front. Then move the hands, placing the left behind the right and parallel. The *R* hands can be used.

STOP: Hit the flat left palm with the little-finger edge of the right flat hand.

YOUNG, YOUTH: Brush the fingertips of both open hands up the chest a few times.

YOUR, YOURS, HIS, HER, THEIR: Push the right flat palm forward toward the person being spoken to. If it is not clear from the context, the *male* or *female* sign can be used first. When using *your* in the plural, push the right flat palm forward, then move it to the right.

 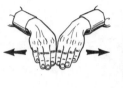 

Wash the floor. Keep the

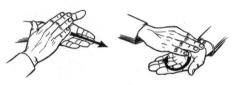

table (bathroom) clean. Wash dishes.

  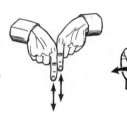 

I need socks (a blanket)

A: Move the right *A* hand in a small arc to the right.
BATHROOM, TOILET: Shake the right *T* hand, palm forward.
BLANKET: Place the open hands in front, palms down. Move them up to shoulder level, ending with *and* hands.
CLEAN, NICE, PURE: Pass the right flat hand over the palm of the left hand.
FLOOR: Hold both flat hands with index fingers touching and pointing forward. Move the hands apart to the sides.
I: Place the right *I* hand on the chest, palm left.
KEEP: Cross the *V* hands at the wrists, right over left.
NEED, HAVE TO, MUST, NECESSARY, SHOULD: Move the right bent index finger down forcefully several times.
SOCKS, HOSE, STOCKINGS: Rub the index fingers alternately against each other as they point down.
TABLE: Place the right flat arm and hand on top of the left flat horizontal arm and hand. Right hand can pat left arm.
THE (definite article): Twist the right *T* hand to the right from a palm-left position.
WASH DISHES, DISHWASHING: Rub the right flat hand in a circle, palms facing.
WASH: Rub the *A* hands together in circular motions.

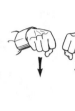  

(a   necktie).   Can   you   sew

   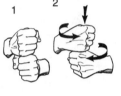

my   skirt   (pants)?   Make

your   bed.   Don't   brag

A: Move the right *A* hand in a small arc to the right.
BED: Put both flat hands together and place them at the right cheek.
BRAG, BOAST, SHOW OFF: Hit the sides of the waist with both extended *A*-hand thumbs a few times.
CAN, ABILITY, ABLE, COMPETENT, COULD, POSSIBLE: Move both *S* (or *A*) hands down together.
DON'T, DOESN'T, DO NOT, NOT: Put the right *A*-

hand thumb under the chin. Move it quickly forward.
MAKE, FIX: Hit the left *S* hand with the right *S* hand. Twist the hands in. Then repeat.
MY, MINE, OWN: Place the right flat hand on the chest.
NECKTIE: Move the right *N* hand around the left *N* hand, then straight down, palm up.
PANTS, SLACKS: Move the curved open hands from below the waist to waist

level, ending with *and* hands.
SEW: Make two *F* hands and pretend to be sewing, moving the right hand up and down a few times near the left hand.
SKIRT: Move the flat open hands down and slightly outward from the waist.
YOU: Point to the person you are signing to. Move the right hand from left to right for more than one person.
YOUR: *(See page 33.)*

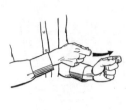   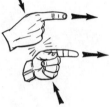

(tease). Be polite (consistent).

I wish (wonder) (suspect).

  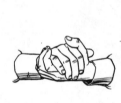 

E d is married (divorced).

BE: Place the right *B* hand at the mouth and move it forward.

CONSISTENT, REGULAR: Form two *G* (or *D*) hands and hit the left hand with the right hand several times as they move forward.

DIVORCE: Place the *D* hands with fingertips touching and swing them apart and sideways, palms forward.

I: Place the right *I* hand on the chest, palm left.

IS: Place right *I* hand at the mouth and move it forward.

MARRIED, MARRIAGE, MARRY: Join the hands with the right above the left, in front of the body.

POLITE, MANNERS: With thumb on chest, pivot the flat open hand forward from the chest or wiggle the fingers.

SUSPECT, SUSPICIOUS: Bend and unbend the right index finger in front of the forehead (or temple) several times, palm in.

TEASE, DAMAGE, PERSE-CUTE, RUIN, SPOIL: Move the right modified *A* hand knuckles over the left modi-fied *A* hand. Repeat several times for *tease*.

WISH: Move the right *C* hand down the chest.

WONDER, CONCERN: Point the index fingers (or *W* hands) at the forehead and rotate them in small oppo-site circles. One hand can be used.

L   y   n   has   two   boys

and   one   girl.   We

 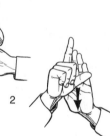 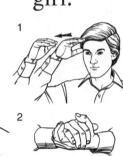 

are   in-laws   (husband   and

AND: Move the right open hand to the right as the hand closes to all fingertips touching.
ARE: Move the right *R* hand forward from the lips.
BOY, MALE: Pretend to be gripping a cap and move the right hand forward a little.
GIRL, FEMALE: Slide the right *A*-hand thumb along the right side of the jaw to the chin.
HAS, HAVE, HAD, OWN,

POSSESS: Move the bent hands fingertips to chest.
HUSBAND: Sign *male* and *marriage*. First pretend to be gripping a cap and move the right hand forward a little. Then join the hands in front of the body, right above left.
IN-LAW: Place the right *and*-hand fingertips into the left *C* hand. Then hold the right *L* hand on the vertical left flat fingers and move the *L* hand down to the palm.

ONE: Hold up the right index finger with palm facing forward.
TWO: Hold up the separated right index and middle fingers with palm facing forward.
WE, US: Touch the right shoulder with the right index finger. Then, circle it forward and back until it touches the left shoulder. The *W* can be used for *we* and *U* for *us*.

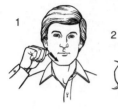 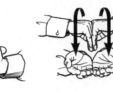 

wife).   How   large

   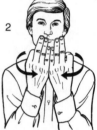

is   your   family?

 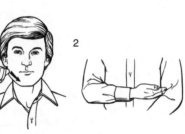 

My   daughter   is

DAUGHTER: Slide the right A-hand thumb along the right side of the jaw to the chin. Then place the right flat hand, palm up, in the fold of the bent left arm.
FAMILY: Hold both F hands facing each other. Then circle both hands forward until little fingers touch.
HOW: Place both bent hands together back to back. Turn them forward until the hands are flat, palms up.

IS: Place right I hand at the mouth and move it forward.
LARGE, BIG: Place both L hands in front of the chest, palms out, and draw them apart.
MY, MINE, OWN: Place the right flat hand on the chest.
WIFE: Move the right A-hand thumb down the right jaw. Next, join both hands in front, right on left.
YOUR, YOURS, HIS, HER, THEIR: Push the right flat palm forward toward the

person being spoken to. If it is not clear from the context, the *male* or *female* sign can be used first. When using *your* in the plural, push the right flat palm forward, then move it to the right.

engaged. I love you. I had

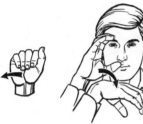  

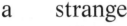

a strange dream. We

 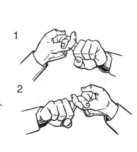

are best friends. Don't

....

ARE: Move the right *R* hand forward from the lips.

BEST: Place the right flat-hand fingertips on the mouth. Slide it off to an *A* hand slightly above the right side of the head.

DON'T, DOESN'T, DO NOT, NOT: Put the right *A*-hand thumb under the chin. Move it quickly forward.

DREAM, DAYDREAM: Place the right index finger on the forehead. Next, bend and unbend the finger as it moves up and forward.

ENGAGED (prior to marriage): Circle the palm-down right *E* hand over the left flat hand and bring it down on the ring finger.

FRIEND, FRIENDSHIP: Hook the right index finger over the left index finger, then reverse the movement.

HAD, HAVE, HAS, OWN, POSSESS: Move the bent-hands fingertips to the chest.

I: Place the right *I* hand on the chest, palm left.

I LOVE YOU: Hold up the right hand with the thumb, index finger, and little finger extended.

STRANGE, ODD: Twist the right *C* hand in front of the face.

WE, US: Touch the right shoulder with the right index finger. Then, circle it forward and back until it touches the left shoulder. The *W* can be used for *we* and *U* for *us*.

tell   the   secret.   Promise

me.   Never.   Where   were

you?   Do   you   need

DO, DID, ACTION, DONE: Move both *C* hands, palms down, in unison to the left then to the right.
ME: Point to or touch the chest with the right index finger.
NEED, HAVE TO, MUST, NECESSARY, SHOULD: Move the right bent index finger down forcefully several times.
NEVER: Move the right flat hand in a half circle at the right. Next, move the hand abruptly away to the right.
PROMISE: Place the vertical right index finger on the lips. Move the right flat hand down to the top of the closed, palm-right left hand.
SECRET, CONFIDENTIAL, PRIVATE: Tap the lips with the right *A*-hand thumb a few times.
TELL, SAY, SPEAK, SPEECH: Move the right index finger in a forward circle from the mouth.
WERE: Hold the right *W*, palm left, to the front. Move it backward as it changes to an *R* hand.
WHERE: Shake the right index finger back and forth.
YOU: Point to the person you are signing to. Move the right hand from left to right for more than one person.

a ride home? Are

you mad? Take care of your

pets. The joke was

A: Move the right *A* hand in a small arc to the right.

ARE: Move the right *R* hand forward from the lips.

HOME: Touch the right *and*-hand fingertips on the mouth, then on the right cheek.

JOKE, FOOL (verb): Hold right bent index finger over nose and pull head down.

MAD, ANGRY, CROSS, MOODY: Bend and unbend the fingers of the right open hand in front of the face a few times.

PET: Stroke the back of the left hand with the fingers of the right hand once or twice.

RIDE (in a vehicle): Make an *O* with the left hand. Place the right curved *U* fingers into it. Move both hands forward.

TAKE CARE OF, SUPER-VISE, CARE: Cross both *V* hands at the wrists, right over left. Move both hands in a circle to the left.

THE (definite article): Twist the right *T* hand to the right

from a palm left position.

WAS: Move right *W* hand backward near right cheek and close it to an *S* hand.

YOU: *(See page 40.)*

YOUR, YOURS, HIS, HER, THEIR: Push the right flat palm forward toward the person being spoken to. If it is not clear from the context, the *male* or *female* sign can be used first. When using *your* in the plural, push the right flat palm forward, then move it to the right.

funny.   Everyone   laughed.

  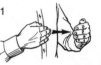 

We   have   good   neighbors.

 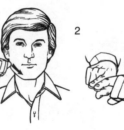 

Your   sister   is

EVERYONE, EVERYBODY: Rub the right A-hand knuckles down the left A-hand thumb a few times. Then sign the number one.
FUNNY, COMICAL: Stroke the tip of the nose with the right U fingers several times.
GOOD, WELL: Touch the lips with the right flat hand. Bring the right hand down into the left hand, palms up.
HAVE, HAD, HAS, OWN, POSSESS: Move the bent-

hands fingertips to the chest.
IS: Place the right I hand at the mouth and move it forward.
LAUGH: Move both extended index fingers from the sides of the mouth up the cheeks a few times.
NEIGHBORS: Move the right curved hand close to the left curved hand. Then move both flat hands down together, palms facing.
SISTER: Slide the thumb of

the extended right A hand along the right side of the jaw. Place both index fingers together.
WE, US: *(See page 39.)*
YOUR, YOURS, HIS, HER, THEIR: Push the right flat palm forward toward the person being spoken to. If it is not clear from the context, the *male* or *female* sign can be used first. When using *your* in the plural, push the right flat palm forward, then move it to the right.

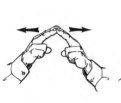

very   pretty.   Buy   a newspaper

(magazine).   My   son

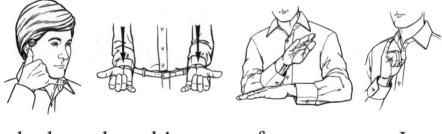

telephoned   this   afternoon.   I

AFTERNOON: Hold the right forearm at a 45-degree angle on the back of the left flat hand, which is horizontal and palm down.

BUY, PURCHASE: Place the right *and* hand in the left hand. Next, move it up and forward or to the right.

I: *(See page 39.)*

MAGAZINE, BOOKLET, BROCHURE, CATALOG, MANUAL: Grasp the bottom edge of the left flat hand between the right index finger and thumb. Slide the right hand along the left hand's edge and little finger.

MY, MINE: *(See page 38.)*

NEWSPAPER: Close the right *G*-hand thumb and index finger and place them into the left flat palm.

PRETTY, BEAUTIFUL: Place the fingertips of the right *and* hand on the chin. Open the hand as it circles the face from right to left. End with the *and* hand near the chin.

SON: Pretend to grip a cap and move the right hand forward a little. Place the right flat hand, palm up, in the crook of the bent left arm.

TELEPHONE, CALL: Hold the thumb of the right *Y* hand to the ear.

THIS: Move both *Y* (or flat) hands down, palms up, at the same time for something abstract.

VERY: Place both *V*-hand fingertips together and move them apart.

   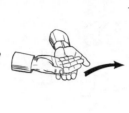  

was	born	deaf.	Are

  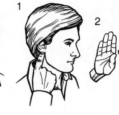

your	parents	deaf?	Do

you	know	sign?	Are

ARE: Move the right *R* hand forward from the lips.

BORN, BIRTH: With palms up, hold the right hand in the left hand and move them forward and up.

DEAF: Point to or touch the right ear with right index finger. Place both flat hands slightly apart, palms forward, and bring together.

DO, DID, ACTION, DONE: Move both *C* hands, palms down, in unison to the left, then to the right.

KNOW, INTELLIGENCE, KNOWLEDGE, RECOGNIZE: Touch the fingertips of the right hand on the forehead several times.

PARENTS: Touch the right temple with the right *P*-hand middle finger, then the right side of the chin.

SIGN (language): Point the index fingers toward each other, palms out, and rotate them in alternating backward circles.

WAS: Move right *W* hand backward near right cheek and close it to an *S* hand.

YOU: Point to the person you are signing to. Move the right hand from left to right for more than one person.

YOUR, YOURS, HIS, HER, THEIR: Push the right flat palm forward toward the person being spoken to. If it is not clear from the context, the *male* or *female* sign can be used first. When using *your* in the plural, push right flat palm forward, then to the right.

you   hearing?   Your   baby's

smile   is   cute.   What

did   she   tell

BABY, INFANT: Pretend to be holding and rocking a baby.
CUTE: Move the right *U* fingertips over the chin a few times.
DID, DO, ACTION, DONE: Move both *C* hands, palms down, in unison to the left, then to the right.
HEARING (person): Move right index finger in a forward circle from the mouth.
IS: Place right *I* hand at the mouth and move it forward.

SHE, HER: Trace the jaw with the right *A*-hand thumb. Then point forward. If the gender is obvious, omit tracing the jaw.
SMILE: Brush the fingers of both hands back across the cheeks, starting near the mouth, and smile.
TELL, SAY, SPEAK, SPEECH: Move the right index finger in a forward circle from the mouth.
WHAT: Move the tip of the right index finger across the

left flat palm.
YOU: Point to the person you are signing to. Move the right hand from left to right for more than one person.
YOUR, YOURS, HIS, HER, THEIR: Push the right flat palm forward toward the person being spoken to. If it is not clear from the context, the *male* or *female* sign can be used first. When using *your* in the plural, push the right flat palm forward, then move it to the right.

you?   They   are   sweethearts.

Congratulations.   B   r   a   d   gave

C   i   n   d   y   a   diamond

A: Move the right *A* hand in a small arc to the right.
ARE: Move the right *R* hand forward from the lips.
CONGRATULATIONS, CONGRATULATE: Touch the mouth with the flat left-hand fingertips and clap several times.
DIAMOND: Put the right *D*-hand fingertips on the ring finger (4th finger) of the flat left hand, palms down.

GAVE, GIVE, DISTRIBUTE: Place the *and* hands in front, palms down, and move the hands forward together, changing to palms-up flat hands.
SWEETHEART, LOVER: Place both *A*-hand knuckles together and move the thumbs up and down together.
THEY, THEM, THESE, THOSE: Point forward or to the people or objects with

the right index finger and move the hand to the right.
YOU: Point to the person you are signing to. Move the right hand from left to right for more than one person.

r   i   n   g.   Are   you

sad?   The   insult   hurt

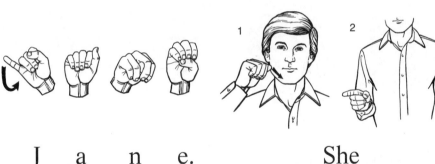

J   a   n   e.   She

....

ARE: Move the right *R* hand forward from the lips.
HURT (emotion): Touch the heart with the right middle finger and twist the hand quickly forward and out.
INSULT: Thrust the right index finger up and forward with a twisting motion to the right.
SAD: Place both open hands in front of the face. Drop both hands several inches while looking sad.
SHE, HER: Trace the jaw with the right *A*-hand thumb. Then point forward. If the gender is obvious, omit tracing the jaw.
THE (definite article): Twist the right *T* hand to the right from a palm-left position.
YOU: Point to the person you are signing to. Move the right hand from left to right for more than one person.

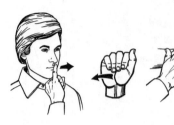 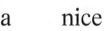  

is   a   nice   person.   They

are   rich   (poor).   The

  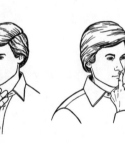

woman   (man)   is   single.

A: Move the right *A* hand in a small arc to the right.
ARE: Move the right *R* hand forward from the lips.
IS: Place the right *I* hand at the mouth and move it forward.
MAN: Place the right open-hand thumb on the forehead and chest.
NICE, CLEAN, PURE: Pass the right flat hand over the palm of the left hand.
PERSON: Move the *P* hands down together.

POOR, POVERTY: Pull the curved right hand off the left elbow, ending with the *and* hand. Repeat several times.
RICH, WEALTHY: Place the back of the right *and* hand in the left palm. Next, lift the right hand straight up as it forms a curved open hand, palms facing.
SINGLE: Circle right vertical index finger, palm in.
THE (definite article): Twist the right *T* hand to the right from a palm-left position.

THEY, THEM, THESE, THOSE: Point forward or to the people or objects with the right index finger and move the hand to the right.
WOMAN: Place the right open-hand thumb on the chin, then on the chest.

Shopping, Money, Numbers, and Colors

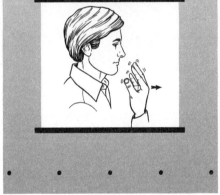

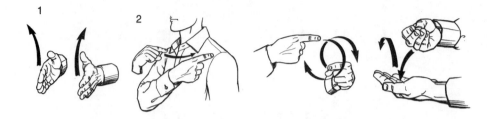

Let's   go   shopping.

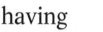

The m a l l is   having   a

special   sale.   What   do   you

A: Move the right *A* hand in a small arc to the right.

DO, ACTION, DID, DONE: Move both downturned *C* hands in unison to left, then to right.

GO: Circle the index fingers around each other as they move forward.

HAVING, HAVE, HAD, HAS, OWN, POSSESS: Move the bent-hands fingertips to the chest.

IS: Place right *I* hand at the mouth and move it forward.

LET: Face both open hands several inches apart. Then move them up and outward together.

SALE, SELL, STORE: Point *and* hands down and move them in and out a few times.

SHOPPING, BUY, PUR-CHASE: Place the right *and* hand in the left hand. Next, move it up and forward or to the right.

SPECIAL, OUTSTANDING, UNIQUE: Hold the left index finger up and grasp it with the right index finger and thumb and pull up.

US, WE: Touch the right shoulder with the right index finger. Then, circle it forward and back until it touches the left shoulder. The *W* can be used for *we* and *U* for *us*.

WHAT: Move the tip of the right index finger across the left flat palm.

YOU: Point to person you are signing to. Move the right hand from left to right if there is more than one person.

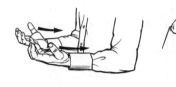  

want to buy? Write

a list. Is the credit card in

your purse? I have

BUY, PURCHASE: Place the right *and* hand in the left hand. Next, move it up and forward or to the right.
CREDIT CARD: Slide the right palm-down *A* hand back and forth across the palm of the flat upturned left hand.
HAVE, HAD, HAS, OWN, POSSESS: Move the bent hands, placing the fingertips on the chest.
I: Place right *I* hand on the chest with palm facing left.

IN: Place right *and* hand fingertips into the left *C* hand.
IS: *(See page 50.)*
LIST: Move the right bent hand down the left flat hand in several small arcs.
PURSE: Hold the right *S* hand at the right side of the body, palm down.
TO: Touch the left vertical index fingertip with the right index fingertip.
WANT, DESIRE: Hold both curved open hands with palms up. Move both hands

toward the body a few times.
WRITE: Pretend to be writing on the left flat palm with the right index finger and thumb.
YOUR, YOURS, HIS, HER, THEIR: Push the right flat palm forward toward the person being spoken to. If it is not clear from the context, the *male* or *female* sign can be used first. When using *your* in the plural, push the right flat palm forward, then move it to the right.

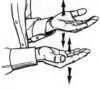

| enough | money. | May | I |

| help | you ? | We | are |

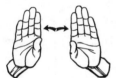

| open | 9 | A. M. | to |

ARE: Move the right *R* hand forward from the lips.
ENOUGH: Move the right flat open hand over the left *S* hand several times.
HELP, AID, ASSIST: Lift the right *S* hand with the left flat hand.
I: Place the right *I* hand on the chest with the palm facing left.
MAY, MAYBE, PERHAPS, POSSIBLY, PROBABLY: Move the flat hands up and down alternately.

MONEY, CAPITAL, FINANCES, FUNDS: Tap the back of the right *and* hand in the left palm a few times.
NINE: Touch the right thumb with the index finger, other fingers extended, and palm forward.
OPEN: Hold both flat-hand palms forward with index and thumbs touching. Move hands apart.
TO: Touch the left vertical index fingertip with the right

index fingertip.
WE, US: Touch the right shoulder with the right index finger. Then, circle it forward and back until it touches the left shoulder. The *W* can be used for *we* and *U* for *us*.
YOU: Point to the person you are signing to. Move the right hand from left to right if there is more than one person.

| 6 | P. | M. | What | are |

| you | looking | for? | Shirt. |

| Blouse. | That | is | new |

ARE: Move the right *R* hand forward from the lips.

BLOUSE: Place the right flat hand with the index finger touching the chest. Move it in a small forward arc ending with the little finger touching the waist area, palm up.

FOR: Place the right index at the right temple. Twist it forward as the hand moves forward.

IS: Place right *I* hand at the mouth and move it forward.

LOOK, LOOK AT, LOOK AT ME, LOOK BACK, LOOK DOWN, OBSERVE, WATCH: Point the right *V* hand to the eyes. Twist the *V* hand and point it forward. For *look at me*, *look back*, and *look down*, point the *V* hand at the eyes, then in the direction needed.

NEW: Brush slightly curved right hand across and over the palm of the left hand.

SHIRT: Pinch the shirt with the right thumb and index

and pull lightly.

SIX: Hold up the right separated index, middle, and ring fingers, palm forward, while touching the tips of the thumb and little finger.

THAT: Place the right *Y* hand in the left palm.

WHAT: Move the tip of the right index finger across the left flat palm.

YOU: Point to the person you are signing to. Move the hand from left to right if there is more than one person.

  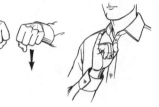

(different)   (ugly).   Can   I

try   this   (these)   on?

The   coat   (shoes)   fit(s)

CAN, ABILITY, ABLE, COMPETENT, COULD, POSSIBLE: Move both *S* (or *A*) hands down together.
COAT, JACKET: Move the *A*-hand thumbs down the chest from near the neck.
DIFFERENT: Cross the index fingers, palms out, and move them to the sides.
FIT, MATCH: Interlock the fingers of the curved open hands; palms face body.
I: Place the right *I* hand on the chest with the palm fac-

ing left.
ON: Place the right flat hand on top of the left flat hand, palms down.
SHOES: Tap the sides of the *S* hands together a couple of times.
THE (definite article): Twist the right *T* hand to the right from a palm-left position.
THESE, THEM, THEY, THOSE: Point forward or to the people or objects with the right index finger and move the hand to the right.

THIS: Place the right index finger in the left flat palm for something specific.
TRY, ATTEMPT, EFFORT: With palms facing, push both *S* hands forward with effort. *Try* and *effort* can be initialized.
UGLY: Cross both index fingers under the nose (other fingers closed) and pull them apart to the sides while bending the index fingers.

perfectly.   I   need   this

  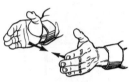

in   a   larger   (smaller)

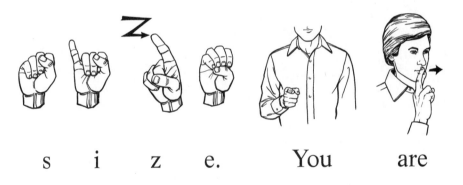

s   i   z   e.   You   are

A: Move the right *A* hand in a small arc to the right.
ARE: Move the right *R* hand forward from the lips.
I: Place the right *I* hand on the chest with the palm facing left.
IN: Place the right *and*-hand fingertips into the left *C* hand.
LARGE, BIG: Place both *L* hands in front of the chest, palms out, and draw them apart.
NEED, HAVE TO, MUST, NECESSARY, SHOULD: Move the right bent index finger down forcefully several times.
PERFECT: Touch both middle finger *P* hands together.
SMALL, LITTLE (measure, size): Place both flat hands with palms facing. Move hands toward each other a few times.
THIS: Place the right index finger in the left flat palm for something specific.
YOU: Point to the person you are signing to. Move the right hand from left to right if there is more than one person.

 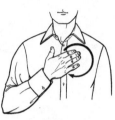 

beautiful.　Please　wrap　this.

Send　the　letter

 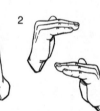 

(package)　soon.　We

BEAUTIFUL, PRETTY:
Place the fingertips of the
right *and* hand on the chin.
Open the hand as it circles
the face from right to left.
End with the *and* hand near
the chin.
LETTER, MAIL: Put the
thumb of the right *A* hand on
the lips; then place it on the
left flat palm.
PACKAGE, BOX: Place vertical flat hands in front, palms
facing. Then change to bent
hands with right over left.

**PLEASE, ENJOY, LIKE,
PLEASURE:** Put the right
hand over the heart and
move it in a small circle.
SEND: Place the right bent-
hand fingertips on the back
of the left bent hand and flip
the fingers forward and up,
ending with a right flat hand.
**SOON, BRIEF, SHORT
(length or time):** Cross the
H hands and slide the right
fingers back and forth over
the left.
THE (definite article): Twist

the right *T* hand to the right
from a palm-left position.
THIS: Place the right index
finger in the left flat palm for
something specific.
WE, US: Touch the right
shoulder with the right index
finger. Then, circle it forward
and back until it touches the
left shoulder. The *W* can be
used for *we* and *U* for *us*.
WRAP: Circle the *W* hands
around each other, then
separate them to the sides.

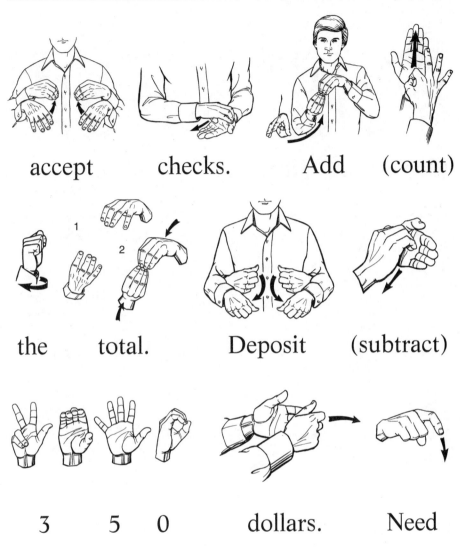

accept   checks.   Add   (count)

the   total.   Deposit   (subtract)

3   5   0   dollars.   Need

ACCEPT: Place the open hands in front. Move them to the chest, closing to *and* hands and ending with fingertips on the chest.
ADD: Place the right open hand to the right, palm down. Place the left *and* hand before the chest. Move the right hand under the left while changing it to an *and* hand, ending with fingertips of both *and* hands touching.
CHECK (bank) Draw the fingertips of right *C* hand,

palm down, across the flat open palm and fingers of the left upturned hand.
COUNT: Move the right *F* thumb and index finger up the flat vertical left hand.
DEPOSIT: Face the *A* hands in front, palms in. Turn the wrists to the sides, so hands separate and point down.
DOLLAR, BILL: Hold the flat left fingers in the right hand and pull the right hand off the left hand several times.
NEED: *(See page 55.)*

SUBTRACT, ABORTION, DEDUCT, REMOVE: Slide right bent-hand fingers down left flat hand. Some end with a closed left *A* or *S* hand.
THE: *(See page 56.)*
THREE HUNDRED FIFTY: Sign three, hundred (point *C* hand forward), five, and zero.
TOTAL, AMOUNT, SUM: Place the open curved hands in front, left above right, and bring them together as they change to *and* hands with fingertips touching.

(don't want) anything? Nothing. I

am satisfied (dissatisfied) with

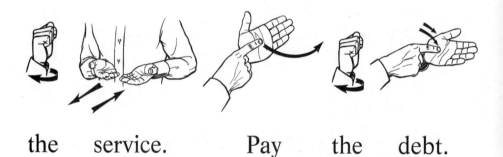

the service. Pay the debt.

AM: Move the right *A*-hand thumb forward from the lips.
ANYTHING: Sign *any* and *thing*. Hold the right *A* hand near the body, palm in. Pivot the hand to the right to a palm-forward position. Drop the right flat hand slightly in front of the body and move it to the right.
DEBT, DUE, OWE: Touch left flat palm with right index finger a few times.
DISSATISFIED, AGGRA-VATED: Hold the fingertips of the right curved open hand on the chest and move the hand in a circular motion or back and forth sideways.
DON'T WANT: Hold both open curved hands palms up and to the front. Turn them over to palms down.
I: Place the right *I* hand on chest with palm facing left.
NOTHING: Hold both *O* hands in front with palms forward. Move them to the sides in opposite directions while simultaneously open-ing both hands.
PAY: Place the right index finger in the left flat palm and move the right index forward.
SATISFIED, SATISFACTION, CONTENT: Hold both flat hands against the chest, right above left, and move them down a few inches together.
SERVICE, SERVE: Move the flat hands back and forth alternately with palms up in front of the body.
WITH: Place both *A* hands together, palms facing.

Both   are   expensive   (cheap).

Get   a   r   e   f   u   n   d.

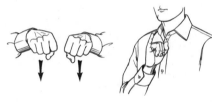  

Can   I   borrow   five dollars

A: Move the right *A* hand in a small arc to the right.
ARE: Move the right *R* hand forward from the lips.
BORROW: Cross the *V* hands in front of the body at the wrists and move them toward self.
BOTH, PAIR: Draw the right *V* fingers down through the left *C* hand, ending with the right *V* fingers touching. Both palms face body.
CAN, ABILITY, ABLE, COMPETENT, COULD,

POSSIBLE: Move both *S* (or *A*) hands down together.
CHEAP, INEXPENSIVE: Move the index-finger side of the right, somewhat curved hand down against the left flat palm.
EXPENSIVE: Hit the back of the right *and* hand into the palm of the left hand. Then move the right hand out to the right while opening it.
FIVE DOLLARS: Hold up the right open hand, palm

forward, and twist it down and up to palm facing the body. This shortcut can be used for signing $1.00-$9.00 dollars, or sign *5* and *dollars*.
GET: Move the open hands together in front of the body with the right hand on top of the left, forming *S* hands.
I: Place the right *I* hand on the chest with the palm facing left.

 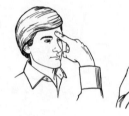 

and ten cents? I like

(hate) that. We are

saving for a house.

AND: Move the right open hand to the right as the hand closes to all fingertips touching.
ARE: Move the right *R* hand forward from the lips.
CENTS, CENT, PENNY: Place the right index finger on the forehead.
FOR: Place the right index at the right temple. Twist it forward as the hand moves forward.
HATE, DESPISE: Flick the middle fingers of both hands forward as the hands move outward together.
HOUSE: Outline the shape of a house with the flat hands.
I: Place the right *I* hand on the chest with the palm facing left.
LIKE, ADMIRE: Hold the thumb and index finger of the right open hand on the chest. Move the hand forward, closing the thumb and index finger.
SAVE: With palms facing in, place the inside of the *V* fingers on the back of the closed left hand.
TEN: Shake the right *A* hand back and forth at the wrist with palm facing left and thumb extended up.
THAT: Place the right *Y* hand in the left flat palm.
WE, US: Touch the right shoulder with the right index finger. Then circle it forward and back until it touches the left shoulder. The *W* can be used for *we* and *U* for *us*.

S   u   e   likes   silver   (gold)

    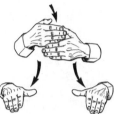

j   e   w   e   l   r   y.   Divide

in   half.   Zero.   Worthless.

DIVIDE: Cross the right hand over the left hand and move both hands down and to the sides, palms down.
GOLD: Touch the right ear with the right index finger. Move the right *Y* hand down and forward and shake it. (*Gold* and *California* are the same sign.)
HALF: Draw the right flat hand across the left flat hand toward the body.
IN: Place right *and* hand fingertips into the left *C* hand.

LIKE, ADMIRE: Hold the thumb and index finger of the right open hand on the chest. Move the hand forward, closing the thumb and index finger.
SILVER: With the right index finger, touch the right ear. Then move the right hand forward, changing to an *S* hand, and shake it.
WORTHLESS, USELESS: Swing the *F* hands together from the sides, palms down. Then move the hands to the

sides as they open.
ZERO: Hold up the right *O* hand with palm facing left.

The   color   is   <u>blue</u>.

Use any sign below.

white.   brown.   gray.   green.

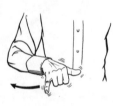   

yellow.   red.   purple.   pink.

BLUE: Shake right *B* hand as it moves to the right.

BROWN: Move the right *B-*hand index finger down the right cheek.

COLOR: Wiggle the fingers of the right open hand in front of the mouth as the hand moves forward.

FIVE: Hold up the right open hand with palm facing forward.

GRAY: Move the open hands back and forth, letting the fingers pass between each other.

GREEN: Shake the right *G* hand as it moves to right.

IS: Place right *I* hand at the mouth and move it forward.

PINK: Move the middle finger of the right *P* hand down over the lips.

PURPLE: Shake the right *P* hand as it moves to right.

RED: Move the right index finger down over the lips.

TWELVE: Hold up the right *S* hand, palm facing self, and flick the index and mid-dle fingers up together.

TWO: Hold up the separated right index and middle finger with palm facing forward.

UNTIL: Touch the right index finger, palm out, to the tip of the left index finger, palm in, in a forward arc.

WHITE: Hold the fingertips of the right curved open hand on the chest and move it forward as it closes to an *and* hand.

YELLOW: Shake the right *Y* hand as it moves to right.

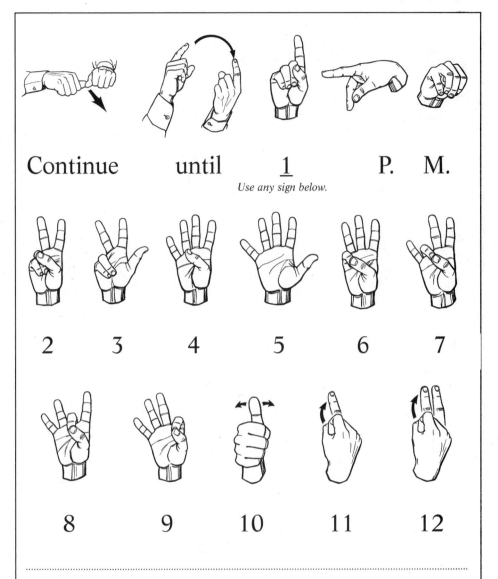

Continue   until   <u>1</u>   P.   M.

Use any sign below.

2   3   4   5   6   7

8   9   10   11   12

CONTINUE, ENDURE: Push the left *A*-hand thumb forward with the right *A* thumb, both palms down.

EIGHT: Hold up the right separated index, ring, and little fingers, palm forward, while touching the tips of thumb and middle finger.

ELEVEN: Hold up the right *S* hand, palm facing self, and flick the index finger up.

FIVE: *(See page 62.)*

FOUR: Hold up the separated right four fingers with thumb bent over palm and palm facing forward.

NINE: Touch the right thumb with the index finger, other fingers extended, and palm forward.

ONE: Hold up the right index finger with palm facing forward.

SEVEN: Hold up the right separated index, middle, and little fingers, palm forward, while touching the tips of the thumb and ring finger.

SIX: Hold up the right sepa-

rated index, middle, and ring fingers, palm forward, while touching the tips of the thumb and little finger.

TEN: Shake the right *A* hand back and forth at the wrist with palm facing left and thumb extended up.

THREE: Hold up the separated right index, middle finger, and thumb with palm facing forward.

TWELVE: *(See page 62.)*

TWO: *(See page 62.)*

UNTIL: *(See page 62.)*

Buy   <u>13</u>   stamps.   14

Use any of the following signs.

15   16   17   18   19

20   21   22   30

BUY, PURCHASE: Place the right *and* hand in the left hand. Next, move it up and forward or to the right.
EIGHTEEN: Hold up right *A* hand, palm left and thumb extended. Twist the wrist forward to an *8* hand.
FIFTEEN: Hold up the right *5* hand, palm facing self, and move all four fingers up and down a few times.
FOURTEEN: Hold up right *4* hand, palm facing self, and move all four fingers up and

down a few times.
NINETEEN: Hold up right *A* hand, palm left and thumb extended. Twist the wrist forward to a *9* hand.
SEVENTEEN: Hold up right *A* hand, palm left and thumb extended up. Twist the wrist forward to a *7* hand.
SIXTEEN: Hold up right *A* hand, palm left and thumb extended up. Twist the wrist forward to a *6* hand.
STAMP (postal): Touch the right *U* fingers to lips and

then on palm of left hand.
THIRTEEN: Hold up the right *3* hand, palm in. Move the index and middle fingers up and down a few times.
TWENTY: Point the extended right index and thumb forward, palm down with other fingers closed, then bring the thumb and index finger together.
TWENTY-ONE: Sign *L-1*.
TWENTY-TWO: Sign *2* then *2* again to right in small arc.
THIRTY: Sign *3* and *O*.

CHAPTER 4

Leisure and Sports

Let's go to

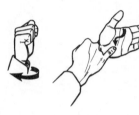

the art museum. The play
drama

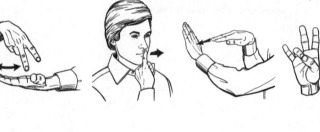

(dance) is at 7 P. M.

ART, ARTIST, DRAW: Draw a wavy line with the right *I* finger over the left flat palm. Use the *person-ending* sign when signing *artist*.

AT: Touch the right flat-hand fingertips against the back of the left flat hand, or fingerspell it.

DANCE: Swing the right *V* fingers back and forth over the left flat hand.

GO: Circle the index fingers around each other as they move forward.

IS: Place the right *I* hand at mouth and move it forward.

LET: Face both open hands several inches apart. Then move them up and outward together.

MUSEUM: Draw the shape of a house with both *M* hands, palms out.

PLAY, DRAMA, ACT, PERFORM, SHOW: Move the *A* hands alternately in circles toward body, palms facing.

SEVEN: Hold up the right separated index, middle, and little fingers, palm forward, while touching the tips of the thumb and ring finger.

THE (definite article): Twist the right *T* hand to the right from a palm-left position.

TO: Touch the left vertical index fingertip with the right index fingertip.

US, WE: Touch the right shoulder with the right index finger. Then, circle it forward and back until it touches the left shoulder. The *W* can be used for *we* and *U* for *us*.

Play pool (Ping-Pong)? Is the

movie interesting? The actors

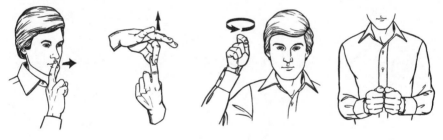

are outstanding. Celebrate with

ACTOR, ACTRESS: Move *A* hands, palms facing, in alternate circles toward the body. Sign *person ending.*
ARE: *(See page 75.)*
CELEBRATE, CHEER, VICTORY: Hold up the right hand with thumb and index finger touching. Move the hand in small circles. Both hands can be used. The *V* hand(s) can be used for *victory.*
INTERESTING, INTEREST: Hold both hands with open

index fingers and thumbs on the chest, other fingers extended, right above left. Move them forward, closing the thumb and index fingers.
IS: *(See page 66.)*
MOVIE: Face the palm of the left open hand almost forward. Place the right open hand on the left hand and move the right hand back and forth.
OUTSTANDING, SPECIAL, UNIQUE: Hold the left index finger up and grasp it with

the right index finger and thumb and pull up.
PING-PONG, TABLE TENNIS: Move the right modified *A* hand back and forth as if playing Ping-Pong.
PLAY, RECREATION: Hold up the *Y* hands. Shake them back and forth at the wrists.
POOL: Move the right *O* hand forward and back toward the left *X* hand as if playing pool.
WITH: Place both *A* hands together, palms facing.

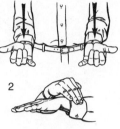

us   tonight.   All   kids

love   fireworks   (magic).   Set up

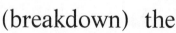

(breakdown)   the   tent.   She

ALL, ENTIRE, WHOLE: Place the left flat hand to the front, palm in. Move the right flat hand, palm forward, around the left while simultaneously turning it until it rests in the left palm.

BREAKDOWN, COLLAPSE: Hold both flat-hand fingertips together in the shape of a pyramid. Maintain contact and bend both hands down, forming a *V* shape.

FIREWORKS: Hold the *S* hands with palms facing forward. Open and close each hand as they move up and down one after another.

KID: Place the extended right hand index and little finger under the nose, palm down, and move the hand up and down slightly.

LOVE: Cross the *S* hands at the wrists over the heart.

MAGIC: Place both *S* hands close to the body and fling them forward and open together several times.

SET UP: Touch both bent-hand fingertips, palms down. Keep fingers touching; move fingertips of both hands up, forming an upside-down *V* shape.

SHE, HER: Trace jaw with right *A*-hand thumb. Point forward.

TENT: Touch the fingertips of both *V* hands together, forming a triangle. Move them down and to the sides.

TONIGHT: Move both *Y* (or flat) hands down, palms up, at the same time. Place right curved hand over left horizontal flat hand and point down.

US, WE: *(See page 66.)*

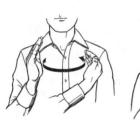

collects   dolls.   He

caught   a   big   fish.

Our   family   is

BIG, LARGE: Place both *L* hands in front of the chest, palms out, and draw them apart.

CAUGHT, CATCH, CAPTURE, GRAB: Quickly move the right curved open hand downward into an *S* hand as it comes to rest on the back of the closed left hand.

DOLL: Hold the right bent index finger across the nose and move the head and hand downward together.

COLLECT, EARN, SALARY, WAGES: Move the right curved hand across the left flat hand. The right hand can end in a closed position.

FAMILY: Hold both *F* hands facing each other. Then circle both hands forward until little fingers touch.

FISH (noun): Hold the left flat-hand fingers at the wrist (or elbow) of the right flat hand. Both hands point forward. Move right hand back and forth from the wrist.

HE, HIM: Pretend to be gripping a cap with the right hand. Move it forward a little. Then point the index finger forward. If the gender is obvious, omit gripping a cap.

IS: Place the right *I* hand at the mouth and move it forward.

OUR: Move the slightly cupped right hand in a semicircle from the right side to the left side of the chest.

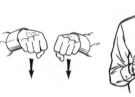

going   camping.   Can   you

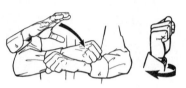

swim?   Throw   (catch)   the

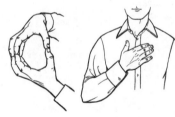

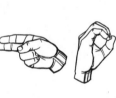

ball.   My   h   o   b   b   y

BALL, ROUND: Touch the fingertips of both curved open hands in the shape of a ball.
CAMP: Make a triangle with both *V*-hand fingers. Move them apart and down to the sides a little. Repeat a few times to the right.
CAN, ABILITY, ABLE, COMPETENT, COULD, POSSIBLE: Move both *S* (or *A*) hands down together.
CATCH, CAPTURE, CAUGHT, GRAB: Quickly

move the right curved open hand downward into an *S* hand as it comes to rest on the back of the closed left hand.
GOING, GO: Circle the index fingers around each other as they move forward.
MY, MINE, OWN: Place the right flat hand on the chest.
SWIM: Point the hands forward and make the motion of swimming.
THROW: Form a right *S* hand near the right side and

throw the hand forward while changing it to an open hand.
YOU: Point to the person you are signing to. Move the right hand from left to right if there is more than one person.

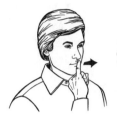  

is   collecting   coins.   That

is   my   favorite   song.

Let's   play cards.   Bring

BRING: Move both open hands either toward self, another person, or in the direction needed, palms up, with one hand a little ahead of the other.

COINS: Draw a small circle with the right index finger in the left flat palm.

COLLECT, EARN, SALARY, WAGES: Move the right curved hand across the left flat hand. The right hand can end in a closed position.

FAVORITE: Touch the chin several times with the right middle finger.

IS: Place the right *I* hand at the mouth and move it forward.

LET, ALLOW: Face both open hands several inches apart. Then move them up and outward together.

MY, MINE, OWN: Place the right flat hand on the chest.

PLAY CARDS, PLAYING CARDS: Pretend to be dealing out cards. Hold the

A-hand thumbs in the crooks of the index fingers with the right hand in front of the left. Move the right hand forward a few times, ending with a palm-up *3* hand.

SONG, MUSIC, HYMN, MELODY, SING: Swing the right flat hand back and forth in front of the left flat hand.

THAT: Place the right *Y* hand in the left flat palm.

US, WE: (See page 66.)

balloons for the children.

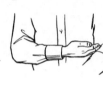

My   son   has

a baseball game tomorrow. The

A: Move the right *A* hand in a small arc to the right.

BALLOON: Hold both *C* hands in front of the mouth with palms facing. Move the hands in a circle until the little fingers touch.

BASEBALL, BAT, SOFTBALL: Make two *S* hands. Place the right on the left and swing forward as if hitting a ball.

CHILDREN, CHILD: Hold the right flat hand in front, palm down, and move the hand up and down as if patting a child's head. Repeat the sign to the left (or right) for more than one child.

FOR: Place the right index at the right temple. Twist it forward as the hand moves forward.

GAME, CHALLENGE: Bring the knuckles of both *A* hands together from the sides of the chest.

HAS, HAVE, HAD, OWN, POSSESS: Move the bent-hands fingertips to chest.

MY, MINE, OWN: Place the right flat hand on the chest.

SON: Pretend to grip a cap and move the right hand forward a little. Place the right flat hand, palm up, in the crook of the bent left arm.

THE (definite article): Twist the right *T* hand to the right from a palm-left position.

TOMORROW: Place the right *A* thumb on the right cheek or chin area and move it forward in an arc.

volleyball   team   needs   you.

I   play   soccer   (football)

(hockey) (basketball).   It   was

BASKETBALL: Move both curved open hands upward and forward.

FOOTBALL: Interlock the open hands in front of the chest a few times, palms down.

HOCKEY: Swing the right *X* finger across the left flat palm several times.

I: Place the right *I* hand on the chest with the palm facing left.

IT: Touch the right *I* finger in the flat left palm.

NEED, HAVE TO, MUST, NECESSARY, SHOULD: Move the right bent index finger down forcefully several times.

PLAY, RECREATION: Hold up the *Y* hands. Shake them back and forth at the wrists.

SOCCER, KICK: Strike the little finger of the left flat hand with the index side of the right hand with an upward swing.

TEAM: Hold both *T* hands with palms facing, then

move them in a circle until the little fingers touch.

VOLLEYBALL: Move both flat hands forward and upward in front of the face.

WAS: Move the right *W* hand backward near the right cheek and close it to an *S* hand.

YOU: Point to the person you are signing to. Move the right hand from left to right if there is more than one person.

a great tennis competition.

B o b hunts deer. Did

you watch the Olympics?

COMPETITION, CONTEST, RACE: Move both *A* hands back and forth alternately in front of body, palms facing.
DEER, ANTLERS: Touch the open-hand thumbs at the temples a few times with palms forward.
DID, ACTION, DO, DONE: Move both *C* hands, palms down, in unison to the left, then to the right.
GREAT, WONDERFUL, EXCELLENT: Push both flat open hands forward and up

several times, palms out.
HUNT, GUN, SHOOT, RIFLE: Pretend to be firing a rifle with the left thumb extended, palm up, and right hand somewhat behind left. Quickly move both hands backward as the right bent index finger is pulled back.
OLYMPICS: Form *F* hands and interlock the thumbs and index fingers a few times as the hands move to right.
TENNIS: Move right *A* hand back and forth as if playing

tennis.
WATCH, LOOK, LOOK AT, LOOK AT ME, LOOK BACK, LOOK DOWN, OBSERVE: Point the right *V* hand to the eyes. Twist the *V* hand and point it forward. For *look at me, look back,* and *look down,* point the right *V* hand at the eyes, then in the direction needed.
YOU: Point to the person you are signing to. Move the right hand from left to right if there is more than one person.

Especially for Divers

Since signing is popular with scuba divers, this section provides a good start. But don't limit yourself to this section only, for there are many signs in this book that can be used as well.

Where   are   the

other   divers?   How   much

time   is   l   e   f   t?   Don't

ARE: Move the right *R* hand forward from the lips.
DIVERS, DIVE: Hold both flat hands palm to palm. Move them together in a forward downward arc.
DON'T, DOESN'T, DO NOT, NOT: Put the right *A*-hand thumb under the chin. Move it quickly forward.
HOW: Place both bent hands together back to back. Turn them forward until the hands are flat, palms up.

IS: Place the right *I* hand at the mouth and move it forward.
MUCH, LOT: With palms facing, hold the open, slightly curved hands in front and move them apart.
OTHER, ANOTHER: Hold the right *A*-hand thumb palm left, and twist it to the right, palm up.
THE (definite article): Twist the right *T* hand to the right from a palm left position.
TIME, CLOCK, WATCH:

Tap the left wrist a few times with the right curved index finger.
WHERE: Shake the right index finger back and forth.

be   careless.   Understand?   Where

 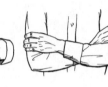 

to   next?   Relax.   Look

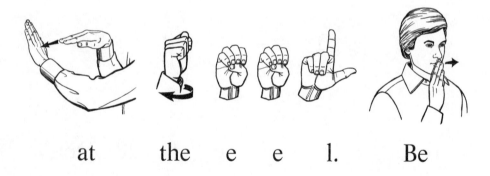

at   the   e   e   l.   Be

AT: Touch the right flat-hand fingertips against the back of the left flat hand, or fingerspell it.
BE: Place right *B* hand at mouth and move it forward.
CARELESS, THOUGHTLESS: Move the right *V* hand back and forth in front of the forehead several times, palm left.
LOOK, LOOK AT, LOOK AT ME, LOOK BACK, LOOK DOWN, OBSERVE, WATCH: Point the right *V* hand to the eyes. Twist the *V* hand and point it forward. For *look at me*, *look back*, and *look down*, point the right *V* hand at the eyes, then in the direction needed.
NEXT: Place flat hands to front, palms in, right behind left. Place the right hand over and ahead of the left.
RELAX, REST: Fold the arms on the chest.
THE (definite article): Twist the right *T* hand to the right from a palm left position.
TO: Touch the left vertical index fingertip with the right index fingertip.
UNDERSTAND, COMPREHEND: Flick up the right index finger in front of the forehead, palm in.
WHERE: Shake the right index finger back and forth.

careful. Beautiful c o r a l.

Stay close to the boat.

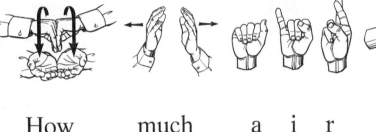

How much a i r do

BEAUTIFUL, PRETTY:
Place the fingertips of the right *and* hand on the chin. Open the hand as it circles the face from right to left. End with the *and* hand near the chin.

BOAT: Move both cupped hands forward in a wavy motion.

CAREFUL: Cross the wrists of both *V* hands in front. Strike the right wrist on the left wrist several times.

CLOSE TO, NEAR, BY: Hold both slightly curved hands to the front and apart, with the right hand near the body. Move the right hand near the left hand.

DO, DID, ACTION, DONE: Move both *C* hands, palms down, in unison to the left, then to the right.

HOW: Place both bent hands together back to back. Turn them forward until the hands are flat, palms up.

MUCH, LOT: With palms facing, hold the open, slightly curved hands in front and move them apart.

STAY, REMAIN: Place the right *A*-thumb tip on left *A*-thumb tip. Push them down together.

THE (definite article): Twist the right *T* hand to the right from a palm left position.

  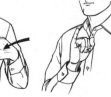 

you   have?   I   am

(almost   out)   confused.   Get

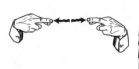  

rope.   Keep   away.   Jump.

ALMOST, NEARLY: With both palms up, move the little-finger edge of the right hand up, hitting the fingertips of the left curved hand.
AM: Move the right *A*-hand thumb forward from the lips.
AWAY: Hold the right curved (or *A*) hand up and move it away from the body to the right. End with the palm facing forward at an upward angle.
CONFUSE, MIX, SCRAMBLE: Circle the right curved open hand, palm down, right to left over the palm-up left curved open hand.
GET: Move the open hands together in front of the body with the right hand on top of the left, forming *S* hands.
HAVE, HAD, HAS, OWN, POSSESS: Move the bent-hands fingertips to the chest.
I: Place the right *I* hand on chest with palm facing left.
JUMP: Place the right *V* fingers on the left flat palm.

Make the *V* jump up and down.
KEEP: Cross the *V* hands at the wrists, right over left.
OUT: Place the right open hand into the left *C* hand and pull it up and out.
ROPE: Hold the *R* hands with fingertips touching. Move them to the sides in a wavy movement.
YOU: Point to the person you are signing to. Move the right hand from left to right if there is more than one person.

  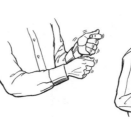 

I   like   <u>fishing</u>.   jogging.

Use any of the following signs.

bicycling.   bowling.   skiing.   canoeing.

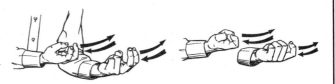

horseback riding. roller skating. ice skating.

BICYCLE, BIKE: Make two *S* hands in front of chest with palms down. Then move them in forward alternating circles as if pedaling.
BOWLING: Swing the right curved open hand forward at the side.
CANOEING: Hold both *S* hands at left side, right on left, and move them together down and backward.
FISHING: Pretend to be holding a fishing rod; move it backward and forward.

HORSEBACK RIDING: Straddle the right *V* fingers over the left *B* hand in front of the body. Move both hands forward in small arcs.
I: Place the right *I* hand on the chest with the palm facing left.
ICE SKATING: Move both *X* hands back and forth alternately in front of the body, palms facing up.
JOGGING: With arms bent, move both partially opened *A* hands back and forth at

the front alternately.
LIKE, ADMIRE: Hold thumb and index finger of the right open hand on chest. Move the hand forward, closing the thumb and index finger.
ROLLER SKATING: Move curved *V* hands, with palms up, back and forth alternately in front of the body.
SKIING: Place both *S* hands at the sides and in front with arms bent. Together, push both hands down and backward.

  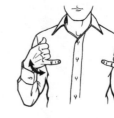

She   plays   the

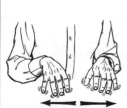  

<u>guitar</u>.   drums.   harp.

Use any of the following signs.

piano.   trombone.   violin.   xylophone.

DRUMS: Hold both modified *A* hands (thumbs in crooks of index fingers) to front. Move them alternately up and down as if playing the drums.

GUITAR: Pretend to be strumming a guitar by holding the left hand up, fingers curled, and moving the right *A* hand up and down.

HARP: Hold the curved open hands to the front and move them backward in circular movements while moving the fingers.

PIANO: Place curved open hands to the front and move them right and left while striking the hands down at imaginary piano keys.

PLAY, RECREATION: Hold up the *Y* hands. Shake them back and forth at the wrists.

SHE, HER: Trace the jaw with the right *A*-hand thumb. Then point forward. If the gender is obvious, omit tracing the jaw.

TROMBONE: Bend the index fingers over the tips of the thumbs (modified *A*

hands). Hold both hands up, the left near the mouth and the right in front of the left. Move the right hand forward and backward.

VIOLIN: Bend the left arm palm up with fingers curled. Move the right *O* hand back and forth over the middle of the left arm.

XYLOPHONE: With palms facing, alternately move the modified *A* hands (thumbs in crooks of index fingers) up and down.

CHAPTER 5

Food
and
Restaurants

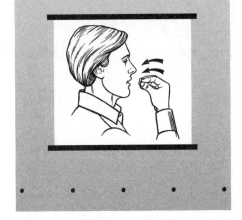

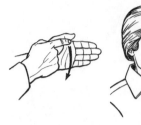 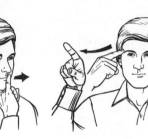 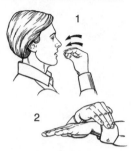

What's for supper

(breakfast)? When do

we eat? Five or

BREAKFAST: Move the fingertips of the right *and* hand to the mouth several times. Next, bend the left arm and rest the left hand in the bend of the right arm. Hold right hand flat and arm bent horizontally. Move right arm upright, palm facing self. **DO:** *(See page 87.)*

EAT, DINE, FOOD, MEAL: Move the fingertips of the right *and* hand to the mouth several times.

FIVE: Hold up right open hand, palm facing forward.

FOR: Place right index at right temple. Twist it forward as hand moves forward.

IS: Place right *I* hand at the mouth and move it forward.

OR, EITHER: Touch the left *L*-hand thumb and index finger several times with the right index finger.

SUPPER, DINNER: Sign *eat* and *night*. Move fingertips of the right *and* hand to the mouth a few times. Next, place right curved hand over flat horizontal left hand.

WE, US: Touch the right shoulder with the right index finger. Then, circle it forward and back until it touches the left shoulder. The *W* can be used for *we* and *U* for *us.*

WHAT: *(See page 90.)*

WHEN: Move the right index finger around the left upright index finger. Then touch the tip of the right index finger on the tip of the left index finger.

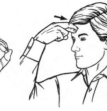 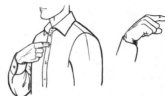

5 : 3   0?   Remind   me   to

buy   bread,   butter,   milk,

  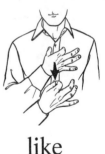

and   eggs.   I   like

AND: Move the right open hand to right as hand closes to all fingertips touching.
BREAD: Place the flat left hand in front of the body. Move the little finger of the right hand down over the back of the left a few times.
BUTTER: Brush the right *H* fingertips across the left flat palm a few times.
BUY, PURCHASE: Place the right *and* hand in the left hand. Next, move it up and forward or to the right.

EGG: Hit the left *H* hand with the right *H* hand; then move both hands down and to the sides.
FIVE-THIRTY: Sign *five* by holding up the right open hand, palm forward. Then, hold up the separated right index, middle finger, and thumb, palm forward. Next, hold up the right *O* hand with palm facing left.
I: Place the right *I* hand on the chest, palm left.
LIKE, ADMIRE: Hold thumb

and index finger of right open hand on chest. Move the hand forward, closing the thumb and index finger.
ME: Point to or touch chest with the right index finger.
MILK: Open and close the *S* hands, one after the other, as they move up and down as if milking a cow.
REMIND: Touch forehead with right *R* hand fingertips.
TO: Touch the left vertical index fingertip with the right index fingertip.

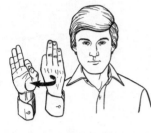

French   toast   with

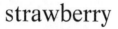

strawberry   jam.   Put   the

juice   in   the   refrigerator.

FRENCH, FRANCE: With the right palm facing the right shoulder, flick or twist the *F* hand until the palm faces forward. Add the sign for *person ending* when referring to a *French* person.

IN: Place the right *and* hand fingertips into the left *C* hand.

JAM, JELLY: Slide the right *J* fingertip across the left palm one or two times.

JUICE: At shoulder level, make a *J* two times with right hand.

PUT, MOVE: Hold the open curved hands to the left front, palms down. Move them together up and down to the right while closing them to *and* hands.

REFRIGERATOR: Shake both *R* hands with palms facing forward.

SOMETHING, SOMEONE, SOMEBODY: Hold the right index finger up with palm facing forward and shake it slightly back and forth from left to right.

STRAWBERRY: Twist the right *and*-hand fingertips and thumb back and forth on the left index finger.

THE (definite article): Twist the right *T* hand to the right from a palm left position.

TOAST: Push the right *V* fingers into the left flat palm, then on the back of the left flat hand.

WITH: Place both *A* hands together, palms facing.

Come   for   dinner   at

6 : 3 0.   Should   I   bring

dessert   (something)?   That   smells

AT: Touch the right flat-hand fingertips against the back of the left flat hand, or finger-spell it.

BRING: Move both open hands either toward self or another person, palms up, with one hand a little ahead of the other.

COME: Circle the index fingers as they move toward the body.

DESSERT: Tap both *D*-hand fingertips together several times.

DINNER: Sign *eat* and *night*. Move the fingertips of the right *and* hand to the mouth a few times. Next, place the right curved hand over the flat horizontal left hand.

FOR: *(See page 82.)*

I: *(See page 83.)*

SHOULD, NEED, HAVE TO, MUST, NECESSARY: Move the right bent index finger down forcefully several times.

SIX-THIRTY: Sign *six* by holding up the right separated index, middle, and ring fingers, palm forward, while touching the tips of the thumb and little finger. Then, hold up separated right index, middle finger, and thumb, palm forward. Next, hold up the right *O* hand with palm facing left.

SMELL, FUMES, ODOR: Move the slightly curved right palm up past the nose a couple of times.

SOMETHING, SOMEONE, SOMEBODY: *(See page 84.)*

THAT: Place the right *Y* hand in the left flat palm.

(tastes)   sour.   I   want

dessert,   too.   I   am

full.   More   milk   and

AM: Move the right *A*-hand thumb forward from the lips.
AND: Move the right open hand to the right as the hand closes to all fingertips touching.
DESSERT: Tap both *D*-hand fingertips together several times.
FULL (physical), FED UP (emotional): Place the back of the right flat hand under the chin.
I: Place the right *I* hand on the chest, palm left.

MILK: Open and close the *S* hands, one after the other, as they move up and down as if milking a cow.
MORE: Bring the right *and* hand up to meet the left *and* hand, fingertips touching.
SOUR: Twist the right index finger forward (or back and forth) at the corner of the mouth several times.
TASTE: Place the right middle finger on the tip of the tongue, other fingers extended.

TOO, ALSO: Place the index fingers together in front with palms down. Then repeat the movement again a little to the left.
WANT, DESIRE: Hold both curved open hands with palms up. Move both hands toward the body a few times.

cookies   anyone?   Do   you

 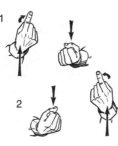  

like   popcorn   with   or

without   butter?   Did   you

ANYONE, ANYBODY: Hold the right *A* hand, palm in, near the body. Pivot the hand to the right to palm forward. Then point up with the index finger.
BUTTER: Brush the right *H* fingertips across the left flat palm a few times.
COOKIE: Twist the right *S-* hand fingertips in the left flat palm. Repeat several times.
DO, DID, ACTION, DONE: Move both *C* hands, palms down, in unison to the left,

then to the right.
LIKE, ADMIRE: Hold the thumb and index finger of the right open hand on the chest. Move the hand forward, closing the thumb and index finger.
OR, EITHER: Touch the left *L*-hand thumb and index finger several times with the right index finger.
POPCORN: Make two *S* hands with palms up. Then flip up the index fingers one after the other.

WITH: Place both *A* hands together, palms facing.
WITHOUT: Bring both *A* hands together, palms facing; then move both hands to the sides while changing them into open hands.
YOU: Point to the person you are signing to. Move the right hand from left to right if there is more than one person.

eat?

What

would

you

like

to

eat?

No

thanks.

Buy

tomatoes,

BUY, PURCHASE: Place the right *and* hand in the left hand. Next, move it up and forward or to the right.

EAT, DINE, FOOD, MEAL: Move the fingertips of the right *and* hand to the mouth several times.

LIKE, ADMIRE: Hold the thumb and index finger of the right open hand on the chest. Move the hand forward, closing the thumb and index finger.

NO: Touch the right middle and index fingers with the thumb.

THANKS, THANK YOU, YOU'RE WELCOME: Smile and bring the fingertips of both flat hands to the lips. Move the hands forward until palms are up. The right hand can be used.

TO: Touch the left vertical index fingertip with the right index fingertip.

TOMATO: Move the right index finger down over the lips. Point the left *and* hand

right. Move the right index finger down and past the fingertips of the left *and* hand.

WHAT: Move the tip of the right index finger across the left flat palm.

WOULD: Move the right *W* hand forward at the right side of face to a *D* hand.

YOU: Point to the person you are signing to. Move the right hand from left to right if there is more than one person.

a   watermelon,   and   grapes.

I   like   to   cook.

Buy   some   bananas,   apples,

AND: Move the right open hand to right as hand closes to all fingertips touching.
APPLE: Touch the right cheek with the right *S*-hand extended index knuckle. Twist it back and forth.
BANANA: Hold up left index finger. Pretend to be peeling a banana with right hand.
BUY, PURCHASE: Place the right *and* hand in the left hand. Next, move it up and forward or to the right.
COOK (verb), FRY, PAN-

CAKE: With palms facing, place the right hand on the left palm. Flip the right hand over, palm up, and rest it on the left hand.
GRAPES: Touch the back of the left hand with the fingertips of the right curved hand. Pick up the right hand and place it on the left hand several times as it moves toward the fingers.
I: Place the right *I* hand on the chest, palm left.
LIKE, ADMIRE: Hold thumb

and index finger of right open hand on chest. Move the hand forward, closing thumb and index finger.
SOME, PART, PORTION: Place the little-finger side of the right curved hand on the left flat palm. Move the right hand toward the body, ending with a right flat hand.
TO: *(See page 88.)*
WATERMELON: Flick the middle finger of the right hand against the back of the closed left hand a few times.

 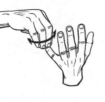  

and   berries.   What   fruit

 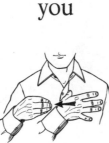  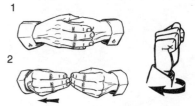

do   you   prefer?   Oranges,

peaches,   and   pears.   The

AND: Move the right open hand to the right as the hand closes to all fingertips touching.

BERRY: Twist the right *and*-hand fingertips and thumb back and forth on the left little finger.

DO, ACTION, DID, DONE: Move both *C* hands, palms down, in unison to the left, then to the right.

FRUIT: Twist the right *F* hand on the right cheek either forward or backward.

ORANGE (color and fruit): Open and close the right *S* hand slightly in front of the mouth once or twice.

PEACH: Place the fingertips of the right open hand on the right cheek and move it down, ending with the *and* hand.

PEAR: Place the right hand over the left *and* hand. Then slide the right hand off while closing it into an *and* hand.

PREFER, RATHER: Hold the right flat hand on the chest and move it up and to the right, changing it to a thumb-up *A* hand.

THE (definite article): Twist the right *T* hand to the right from a palm left position.

WHAT: Move the tip of the right index finger across the left flat palm.

YOU: Point to the person you are signing to. Move the right hand from left to right if there is more than one person.

blueberries (blackberries) are ripe.

I am thirsty. Would

you like a drink?

A: Move the right *A* hand in a small arc to the right.
AM: Move the right *A*-hand thumb forward from the lips.
ARE: Move the right *R* hand forward from the lips.
BLACKBERRY: Move the right index finger across the right eyebrow from left to right. Hold the left little finger with the right *and* hand and twist back and forth.
BLUEBERRY: Shake the right *B* hand as it moves to the right. Hold the left little finger with the right *and* hand. Twist back and forth.
DRINK: Move the right *C* hand to the mouth as if holding a glass.
I: Place the right *I* hand on the chest, palm left.
LIKE, ADMIRE: Hold the thumb and index finger of the right open hand on the chest. Move the hand forward, closing the thumb and index finger.
RIPE, SOFT: Move the curved open hands down to *and* hands a few times.
THIRSTY: Move the right index finger from under the chin and down the neck.
WOULD: Move the right *W* hand forward at the right side of face to a *D* hand.
YOU: Point to the person you are signing to. Move the right hand from left to right if there is more than one person.

   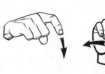

The   lady   needs   a

fork,   spoon,   and   knife.

The   glasses   and   plates

A: Move the right *A* hand in a small arc to the right.

AND: Move the right open hand to the right as the hand closes to all fingertips touching.

FORK: Jab the flat left palm with the fingers of the right *V* hand several times.

GLASS (drinking): Place the right *C* hand in the left flat palm and raise the *C* hand up off the flat hand a little.

KNIFE: Slide the right *H* (or index) fingers across and off the left *H* (or index) fingers a few times.

LADY: Slide the right *A*-hand thumb along the right side of the jaw to the chin. Then, hold the thumb of the right open flat hand on the chest and move it up and forward.

NEED, HAVE TO, MUST, NECESSARY, SHOULD: Move the right bent index finger down forcefully several times.

PLATE: With both hands, form a circle with the thumbs and fingers.

SPOON: Scoop the curved right *H* fingers into the slightly curved left palm and move the right hand up toward the mouth a few times.

THE (definite article): Twist the right *T* hand to the right from a palm-left position.

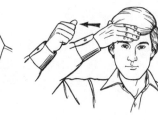

match.   I   forgot   cups

(napkins).   Boil   the   water.   Mom

baked   a   chocolate   cake.

BAKE, OVEN: Hold the left flat hand to the front, palm down, and slide the right, palm-up, flat (or *B*) hand under the left.

BOIL, COOK (verb): Hold the horizontal left arm in front, palm down, and wiggle the fingers of the right curved hand under the left palm.

CAKE: Move the right *C*-hand fingertips across the left flat hand.

CHOCOLATE: Circle the right *C* hand over the left flat hand.

CUP: Place the right *C* hand, little finger down, on the flat left hand.

FORGOT, FORGET, FORSAKE: Move the right open hand, palm in, across the forehead from left to right, ending with the *A* hand to the right of the head.

I: Place the right *I* hand on the chest, palm left.

MATCH, FIT: Interlock the fingers of the curved open hands, palms facing body.

MOM, MOTHER: Touch the thumb of the right open hand against the chin.

NAPKIN: Wipe the mouth with the fingertips of the right hand.

THE (definite article): Twist the right *T* hand to the right from a palm left position.

WATER: Touch the right side of the mouth a couple of times with the right *W* index finger.

Where   is   a   good

restaurant?   Is   the   food

expensive?   We   ate   there

A: Move the right *A* hand in a small arc to the right.
ATE, FOOD, DINE, MEAL: Move the fingertips of the right *and* hand to the mouth several times.
EXPENSIVE: Hit the back of the right *and* hand into the palm of left hand. Then move the right hand out to the right while opening it.
FOOD, DINE, EAT, MEAL: Move the fingertips of the right *and* hand to the mouth several times.

GOOD, WELL: Touch the lips with the right flat hand. Bring the right hand down into the left hand, palms up.
IS: Place the right *I* hand at the mouth. Move it forward.
RESTAURANT: Move the right *R* fingers from the right to the left of the mouth.
THE (definite article): Twist the right *T* hand to the right from a palm-left position.
THERE: Point with the right index finger to an imaginary object.

WE, US: Touch the right shoulder with the right index finger. Then, circle it forward and back until it touches the left shoulder. The *W* can be used for *we* and *U* for *us*.
WHERE: Shake the right index finger back and forth, palm forward.

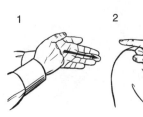  

last week.   Apple   pie

   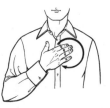

and   vanilla   ice cream,   please.

I   did   not   order

AND: Move the right open hand to the right as the hand closes to all fingertips touching.

APPLE: Touch the right cheek with the right *S*-hand extended index knuckle. Twist it back and forth.

DID, ACTION, DO, DONE: Move both *C* hands, palms down, in unison to the left, then to the right.

I: Place the right *I* hand on the chest, palm left.

ICE CREAM, LOLLIPOP: Twist the right *S* hand down near the mouth as if licking an ice cream cone.

LAST WEEK: Slide the right index finger forward over the left flat palm. Keep the right hand moving up and back until the index points over the right shoulder.

NOT, DOESN'T, DON'T, DO NOT: Put the right *A*-hand thumb under the chin. Move it quickly forward.

ORDER, COMMAND: Point to the mouth with the right index finger. Then quickly twist it forward and slightly down with force.

PIE: Slide the little finger of the right flat hand over the left flat palm two times, each at different angles.

PLEASE, ENJOY, LIKE, PLEASURE: Put the right hand over the heart and move it in a small circle.

VANILLA: Shake the right *V* hand back and forth.

this.   They   ordered   meat,

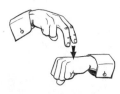

potatoes,   and   vegetables.   Doughnuts

and   black   coffee,   please.

AND: Move the right open hand to the right as the hand closes to all fingertips touching.

BLACK: Move the right index finger across the right eyebrow from left to right.

COFFEE: Hold *S* hands forward and move the right hand in a circle over the left.

DOUGHNUT: Place the *R* hands at each side of the mouth and move them in an outward circle until they meet.

MEAT, BEEF, FLESH: Squeeze the flesh between the index and thumb of the left hand with the index and thumb of the right hand.

ORDER, COMMAND: Point to the mouth with the right index finger. Then quickly twist it forward and slightly down with force.

PLEASE, ENJOY, LIKE, PLEASURE: Put the right hand over the heart and move it in a small circle.

POTATO: Tap the curved right *V* fingertips on the back of the left *S* hand.

THEY, THEM, THESE, THOSE: Point forward or to the people or objects with the right index finger and move the hand to the right.

THIS: Place the right index finger in the left flat palm for something specific.

VEGETABLE: Place the right *V* index finger palm forward on right cheek and twist the wrist to the left.

Do	you	have	any

gum	(candy)	(peanuts)?	I

 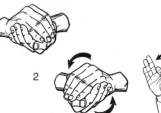 

want	a	hamburger,	french fries,

A: Move the right *A* hand in a small arc to the right.

ANY: Hold the right *A* hand with palm in and pointing left. Swing it to a palm forward position.

CANDY: Move the right *U* fingertips down the lips and chin a few times.

DO, DID, ACTION, DONE: Move both *C* hands, palms down, in unison to the left, then to the right.

FRENCH FRIES: Sign *F* with the right hand and move it to the right.

GUM (chewing): Place the right *V* fingertips on the cheek. Bend and straighten the *V* fingers a few times.

HAMBURGER: Place the right cupped hand on the left cupped hand, then reverse.

HAVE, HAD, HAS, OWN, POSSESS: Move the bent-hands fingertips to the chest.

I: Place the right *I* hand on the chest, palm left.

PEANUTS, NUTS: Place the thumb of the right *A* hand behind the upper teeth and quickly move it forward.

WANT, DESIRE: Hold both curved open hands with palms up. Move both hands toward the body a few times.

YOU: Point to the person you are signing to. Move the right hand from left to right for more than one person.

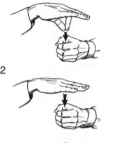

and soda. Do you

want this to go?

I don't like beer.

AND: Move right open hand to the right as hand closes to all fingertips touching.
BEER: Move the right *B* hand down the right side of the mouth.
DO, DID, ACTION, DONE: Move both *C* hands, palms down, in unison to the left, then to the right.
DON'T, DOESN'T, DO NOT, NOT: Put the right *A*-hand thumb under the chin. Move it quickly forward.
GO: Circle the index fingers around each other as they move forward.
I: Place the right *I* hand on the chest, palm left.
LIKE, ADMIRE: Hold the thumb and index finger of the right open hand on the chest. Move the hand forward, closing the thumb and index finger.
SODA, POP: Place right index finger and thumb of *F* hand into the left *O* hand. Next, hit the left *O* hand with the right open hand.

THIS: Place the right index in the left flat palm for something specific.
TO: Touch the left vertical index fingertip with the right index fingertip.
WANT, DESIRE: Hold both curved open hands with palms up. Move both hands toward the body a few times.
YOU: Point to person you are signing to. Move the right hand from left to right if there is more than one person.

Where   is   the   restroom

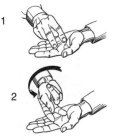  

(kitchen)?   A   table   for

two   in   a   no   smoking

A: Move the right *A* hand in a small arc to the right.
FOR: Place right index at right temple. Twist it forward as the hand moves forward.
IN: Place the right *and*-hand fingertips into the left *C* hand.
IS: Place right *I* hand at the mouth and move it forward.
KITCHEN: Put the right *K* hand, with its palm down, in the left palm, repeat action with palm up.
NO: Touch the right middle and index fingers with the thumb.
RESTROOM: Move the right *R* hand to the right in a small arc.
SMOKING: Place the right *V* fingers, palm in, in front of the lips.
TABLE: Place the right flat arm and hand on top of the left flat horizontal arm and hand. Right hand can pat left arm.
THE (definite article): Twist the right *T* hand to the right from a palm-left position.
TWO: Hold up the separated right index and middle finger with palm facing forward.
WHERE: Shake the right index finger back and forth, palm forward.

area. I will be

 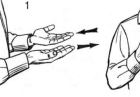  

your waiter. May

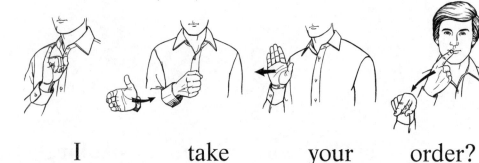

I take your order?

AREA, LOCATION, PLACE: Touch the *P*-hand fingers, palms facing, to the front and move them back in opposite semicircles, touching fingers again near the body. *Area, location,* and *place* may be initialized.

BE: Place the right *B* hand at the mouth and move it forward.

I: Place the right *I* hand on the chest, palm left.

MAY, MAYBE, PERHAPS, POSSIBLY, PROBABLY: Move the flat hands up and down alternately.

ORDER, COMMAND: Point to the mouth with the right index finger. Then quickly twist it forward and slightly down with force.

TAKE: Move the right open hand from right to left, ending with a closed hand near the body.

WAITER, WAITRESS: Move the flat hands alternately back and forth with palms up. Add *person-ending* sign.

WILL (verb), SHALL, WOULD: Hold the flat hand to the right side of the face and move it forward.

YOUR, YOURS, HIS, HER, THEIR: Push the right flat palm forward toward the person being spoken to. If it is not clear from the context, the *male* or *female* sign can be used first. When using *your* in the plural, push the right flat palm forward, then move it to the right.

| Do | you | drink | wine |

  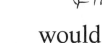 

| (liquor)? | I | would | like |

| spaghetti | and | salad | for |

AND: Move the right open hand to right as hand closes to all fingertips touching.

DO, DID, ACTION, DONE: Move both *C* hands, palms down, in unison to the left, then to the right.

DRINK: Move the right *C* hand to the mouth as if holding a glass.

FOR: Place the right index at the right temple. Twist it forward as the hand moves forward.

I: Place the right *I* hand on the chest, palm left.

LIKE, ADMIRE: Hold the thumb and index finger of the right open hand on the chest. Move the hand forward, closing the thumb and index finger.

LIQUOR, WHISKEY: Extend the index and little finger of the right hand and hit the back of the left *S* hand a few times with the little finger of the right hand.

SALAD: Twist *V* hands up a few times.

SPAGHETTI, STRING, THREAD, WIRE: Touch the *I* fingers. Then move them apart as they make little circles.

WINE: Move right *W* hand over the right cheek in a forward circular movement.

WOULD: Move the right *W* hand forward at the right side of face to a *D* hand.

YOU: Point to person you are signing to. Move the right hand from left to right if there is more than one person.

lunch.   Coffee   with

cream   and   sugar.   The

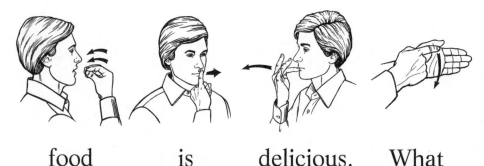

food   is   delicious.   What

AND: Move the right open hand to the right as the hand closes to all fingertips touching.
COFFEE: Hold both *S* hands forward and move the right hand in a circle over the left.
CREAM: Slide the curved right hand across the flat left hand.
DELICIOUS: Place the right middle finger on the lips, other fingers extended. Then move hand forward.

FOOD, DINE, EAT, MEAL: Move the fingertips of the right *and* hand to the mouth several times.
IS: Place the right *I* hand at the mouth and move it forward.
LUNCH: Sign *eat* and *noon*. First move the fingertips of the right *and* hand to the mouth several times. Then, bend the left arm and hold the left flat hand horizontal. Place the bent vertical right arm elbow on the fingertips

of the left hand.
SUGAR, SWEET: Move the right fingertips down over the lips (or the chin, as some prefer.)
THE (definite article): Twist the right *T* hand to the right from a palm left position.
WHAT: Move the tip of the right index finger across the left flat palm.
WITH: Place both *A* hands together, palms facing.

do you want on

your sandwich? A little

salt and pepper. No

A: Move the right *A* hand in a small arc to the right.
AND: Move right open hand to the right as hand closes to all fingertips touching.
DO, DID, ACTION, DONE: Move both *C* hands, palms down, in unison to the left then to the right.
LITTLE (quantity, amount): Rub the tips of the right index finger and thumb together.
NO: Touch the right middle and index fingers with the thumb.

ON: Place the right flat hand on top of the left flat hand, palms down.
PEPPER: Shake the right *O* hand up and down as it points downward.
SALT: Tap the top of the left *H* fingers with the right *V* fingers a few times.
SANDWICH: Put both flat hands together near mouth.
WANT, DESIRE: Hold both curved open hands with palms up. Move both hands toward the body a few times.

YOU: Point to the person you are signing to. Move the right hand from left to right if there is more than one person.
YOUR, YOURS, HIS, HER, THEIR: Push the right flat palm forward toward the person being spoken to. If it is not clear from the context, the *male* or *female* sign can be used first. When using *your* in the plural, push the right flat palm forward, then move it to the right.

onions.　　This　restaurant　is　world

famous.　The　　chef　　is

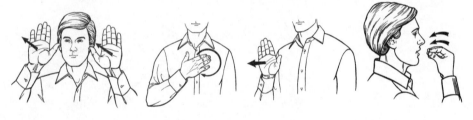

wonderful.　Enjoy　your　meal.

CHEF, COOK (noun): Hold both flat hands to the front, palm to palm with right on left. Flip right hand over on the upturned left palm. Add the sign for *person ending*.
MEAL, EAT, DINE, FOOD: Move fingertips of right *and* hand to mouth several times.
FAMOUS, FAME: Place both index fingers at the mouth and roll them out and up in small spirals.
IS: *(See page 102.)*
ONION: Place the knuckle of

the right bent index finger at the corner of the right eye. Twist it back and forth.
ENJOY, PLEASE, LIKE, PLEASURE: Put the right hand over the heart and move it in a small circle.
RESTAURANT: Move the right *R* fingers from the right to the left of the mouth.
THIS: *(See page 98.)*
WONDERFUL, EXCELLENT, FANTASTIC: Push both flat open hands forward and up several times, palms out.

WORLD: With the right *W* hand, make a forward circle around the left *W* hand, ending with the right resting on top of the left.
YOUR, YOURS, HIS, HER, THEIR: Push the right flat palm forward toward the person being spoken to. If it is not clear from the context, the *male* or *female* sign can be used first. When using *your* in the plural, push the right flat palm forward, then move it to the right.

Are   you   hungry   for

pizza?   cheese?   chicken   soup?

Use any of the following signs.

corn?   pancakes?   biscuits?   crackers?

ARE: Move the right *R* hand forward from the lips.
BISCUIT: Hold the thumb and fingertips of right *C* hand in the left flat palm and raise the right hand several times.
CHEESE: Twist the heels of both open hands against each other.
CHICKEN: Hold the open thumb and index at mouth and open and close them. Some add a pecking motion on left flat hand with right

closed thumb and index.
CORN: Place the right index finger in front of the mouth and twist it back and forth.
CRACKER: Hit the right *S* hand close to the left elbow.
FOR: Place the right index finger at the right temple. Twist it forward as the hand moves forward.
HUNGRY, CRAVE, STARVE: Move the right *C* hand down the chest.
PANCAKE, COOK, FRY (verb): With palms facing,

place the right hand on the left palm. Flip the right hand over, palm up, and rest it on the left hand.
PIZZA: Draw a *Z* shape in the air with the right *P* hand.
SOUP: Push the slightly curved *H* fingers into and up from the left curved hand a few times.
YOU: Point to the person you are signing to. Move the right hand from left to right if there is more than one person.

What will the <u>turkey</u>

Use any sign below.

cost? pineapple lemon cabbage

 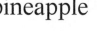  

bacon oil syrup beef

BACON: Touch the fingertips of the *U* hands in front of the chest. Move hands apart in wavy movements.

BEEF, MEAT, FLESH: Squeeze the flesh between the index and thumb of the left hand with the index and thumb of the right hand.

CABBAGE: Hit the sides of the head simultaneously with both *A* (or *S*) hands.

COST, CHARGE, FINE, PRICE, TAX: Hit the right bent index finger across and down the left palm.

LEMON: Place the right *L*-hand thumb on the lips. Make an expression appropriate for a sour taste.

OIL, FAT, GRAVY, GREASE: Place left hand, palm in, and hold the lower edge of the left palm with the right thumb and index fingers. Move the right hand down several times.

PINEAPPLE: Place the middle finger of the right *P* hand on the cheek and twist

hand forward.

SYRUP, MOLASSES: Drag the right index finger across the lips from left to right.

TURKEY: Shake the right *Q* hand in front of the mouth. Move it forward and down with a wavy movement.

WHAT: Move the tip of the right index finger across the left flat palm.

WILL (verb), SHALL, WOULD: Hold the right flat hand to the right side of the face and move it forward.

CHAPTER 6

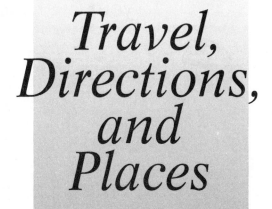

Travel, Directions, and Places

When   is   your   vacation?

Where   are   you   going?

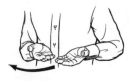 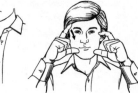

Bring   your   camera.   Take

ARE: Move the right *R* hand forward from the lips.

BRING: Move both open hands either toward self, another person, or in the direction needed, palms up, with one hand a little ahead of the other.

CAMERA: Place both open thumb and bent index fingers before the face with all other fingers closed. Move the right index finger up and down.

GO: Circle the index fingers around each other as they move forward.

IS: Place right *I* hand at the mouth and move it forward.

TAKE: Move the right open hand from right to left, ending with a closed hand near body.

VACATION, HOLIDAY, LEISURE: Place the thumbs at the armpits and wiggle the fingers.

WHEN: Move the right index finger around the left upright index finger. Then touch the tip of the right index finger on the tip of the left index finger.

WHERE: Shake the right index finger back and forth.

YOU: *(See page 121.)*

YOUR, YOURS, HIS, HER, THEIR: Push the right flat palm forward toward the person being spoken to. If it is not clear from the context, the *male* or *female* sign can be used first. When using *your* in the plural, push the right flat palm forward, then move it to the right.

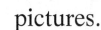

lots   o f   pictures.   Help

me   carry   these   things.

My   car   needs   gasoline.

CAR, DRIVE: Make two *S* hands. Pretend to be steering a car.

CARRY, TRANSPORT: Move the slightly curved hands together from right to left (or left to right) in a small arc, palms up.

GASOLINE: Move the right *A*-hand thumb into the left *O* hand.

HELP, AID, ASSIST: Lift the right *S* hand with the left flat hand.

LOTS, MANY: Place the palm-up *S* hands in front and throw them up together into open hands a couple of times.

ME: Point to or touch the chest with right index finger.

MY, MINE, OWN: Place the right flat hand on the chest.

NEED, HAVE TO, MUST, NECESSARY, SHOULD: Move the right bent index finger down forcefully several times.

PICTURE, PHOTOGRAPH: Move the right *C* hand from the right cheek and place it against the left vertical flat hand.

THESE, THEM, THEY, THOSE: Point forward or to the people or objects with the right index finger and move the hand to the right.

THING: Drop the right flat hand slightly in front of the body and move it to the right.

Come   with   us   to   the

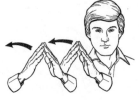   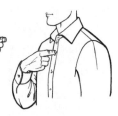

city.   You   persuaded   me.

Drive   slower   (faster).   Which

CITY, COMMUNITY, TOWN, VILLAGE: Touch both flat-hand fingertips together forming a triangle. Repeat a couple of times as hands move to the right.
COME: Circle the index fingers as they move toward the body.
DRIVE, CAR: Make two *S* hands like steering a car.
FAST, QUICK: Flip the right thumb from the bent index.
ME: *(See page 109.)*
PERSUADE, URGE: Place

the modified *A* hands (thumbs in crooks of bent index fingers) to the front, the right slightly behind the left. Draw the hands back and forth, getting closer to the body each time.
SLOW: Slide the right hand slowly over back of left hand from fingertips to wrist.
TO: Touch the left vertical index fingertip with the right index fingertip.
US, WE: Touch the right shoulder with the right index

finger. Then, circle it forward and back until it touches the left shoulder. The *W* can be used for *we* and *U* for *us*.
WHICH, WHETHER: Face *A* hands palm to palm in front of the chest and move them alternately up and down.
WITH: Place both *A* hands together, palms facing.
YOU: Point to the person you are signing to. Move the right hand from left to right if there is more than one person.

| way? | Get | the | m a p. |

| What | time | should | we |

| be | there? | Park | (lock) |

BE: Place the right *B* hand at the mouth and move it forward.

GET: Move the open hands together in front of the body with the right hand on top of the left, forming *S* hands.

LOCK, KEY, LOCK UP: Twist the right bent index finger to the right on the left flat palm.

PARK (a vehicle): Place the right *3* hand on top of the left flat palm with fingers pointing forward.

SHOULD, NEED, HAVE TO, MUST, NECESSARY: Move the right bent index finger down forcefully several times.

THE (definite article): Twist the right *T* hand to the right from a palm-left position.

THERE: Point with the right index finger to an imaginary object.

TIME, CLOCK, WATCH: Tap the left wrist a few times with the right curved index finger.

WAY, STREET, AVENUE, HIGHWAY, PATH, ROAD: Face both flat hands palm to palm and move them forward in a winding movement.

WE, US: Touch the right shoulder with the right index finger. Then, circle it forward and back until it touches the left shoulder. The *W* can be used for *we* and *U* for *us*.

WHAT: Move the tip of the right index finger across the left flat palm.

(empty) the car. The

airplane leaves (arrives) in

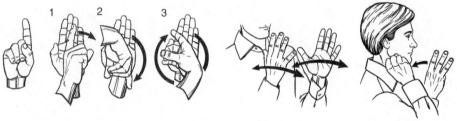

one hour. Traffic was

AIRPLANE, FLY, JET: Move the right *Y* hand, with index finger extended, forward and up.
ARRIVE, GET TO, REACH: Move the right curved hand forward into the palm of the left curved hand, palms face self.
CAR, DRIVE: Make two *S* hands. Pretend to be steering a car.
EMPTY, NUDE, VACANT: Slide the right middle finger over the back of the flat left

hand from the wrist past the knuckles.
HOUR: Rotate the right *D* hand in a circle on the left flat hand.
IN: Place the right *and*-hand fingertips into left *C* hand.
LEAVE, DEPART, RETIRE: Hold both flat hands to the right, palms down, and draw them up to self, ending in *A* hands.
ONE: Hold up the right index finger with palm facing forward.

THE (definite article): Twist the right *T* hand to the right from a palm-left position.
TRAFFIC: Move the open hands, palms facing, alternately back and forth several times.
WAS: Move the right *W* hand backward near the right cheek and close it to an *S* hand.

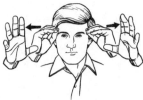   

terrible.   I   got   lost.

Is   the   train   on

  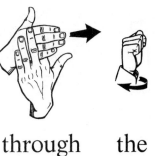

time?   Go   through   the

GO: Circle the index fingers around each other as they move forward.
GOT, GET: Move the open hands together in front of the body with the right hand on top of the left, forming *S* hands.
I: Place the right *I* hand on the chest, palm left.
IS: Place the right *I* hand at the mouth and move it forward.
LOST, LOSE: Touch the fingertips of both *and* hands.

Then drop them as the hands open.
ON: Place the right flat hand on top of the left flat hand, palms down.
TERRIBLE, AWFUL, FEARFUL, TRAGIC: Hold the *O* hands at the temples and fling the fingers forward to open hands, palms facing.
THE (definite article): Twist the right *T* hand to the right from a palm-left position.
THROUGH: Slide the right

flat hand between the left index and middle fingers.
TIME, CLOCK, WATCH: Tap the left wrist a few times with the right curved index finger.
TRAIN, RAILROAD: Rub the right *H* fingers over the left *H* fingers, palms down, several times.

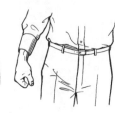

| gate. | My | suitcase | is |

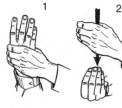

| gone | (full). | What | is |

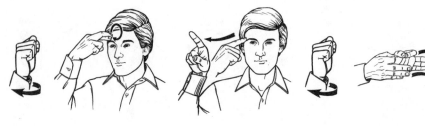

| the | reason | for | the | delay? |

DELAY, PROCRASTINATE: Place the *F* hands in front and move them forward in small arcs with palms facing.

FOR: Place the right index at the right temple. Twist it forward as the hand moves forward.

FULL, FILLED: Pass the right flat hand to the left over the index side of the closed left hand.

GATE: Hold both flat hands with fingertips facing. Swing the right hand back and forth like a gate several times.

GONE, ABSENT: Pull the right open hand down through the left *C* hand. The right hand ends in an *and* hand. The left hand can close to an *O* hand.

IS: Place the right *I* hand at the mouth and move it forward.

MY, MINE, OWN: Place the right flat hand on the chest.

REASON: With the right *R* hand, make a circle in front of the forehead.

SUITCASE: Imitate picking up a suitcase with the right *S* hand.

THE (definite article): Twist the right *T* hand to the right from a palm-left position.

WHAT: Move the tip of the right index finger across the left flat palm.

| May | I | have | this |

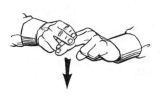 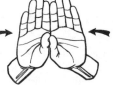 

| seat? | Close | the | window. |

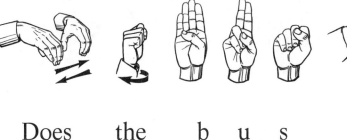

| Does | the | b | u | s | go |

CLOSE, SHUT: Place both flat hands palms forward, slightly apart, and bring together.
DOES, DO, ACTION, DID, DONE: Move both *C* hands, palms down, in unison to the left, then to the right.
GO: Circle the index fingers around each other as they move forward.
HAVE, HAD, HAS, OWN, POSSESS: Move the bent-hands fingertips to the chest.

I: Place the right *I* hand on the chest, palm left.
MAY, MAYBE, PERHAPS, POSSIBLY, PROBABLY: Move the flat hands up and down alternately.
SEAT, BE SEATED, SIT: Hold the right *H* fingers on the left *H* fingers and push both hands down a little.
THE (definite article): Twist the right *T* hand to the right from a palm-left position.
THIS: Place the right index finger in the left flat palm for

something specific.
WINDOW: Place the right flat hand on the left flat hand and move the right up a little, palms face in.

there   everyday?   Where   is

the   b   u   s   stop?   Where

do   I   change

CHANGE, ADJUST: With palms facing, hold up the modified *A* hands (thumbs in crooks of index fingers), right over left. Twist the hands so they switch places.
EVERYDAY, DAILY: Put the right *A* hand on the right cheek and slide it forward a few times.
DO, ACTION, DID, DONE: Move both *C* hands, palms down, in unison to the left, then to the right.

I: Place the right *I* hand on the chest, palm left.
IS: Place the right *I* hand at the mouth and move it forward.
STOP: Hit the flat left palm with the little-finger edge of the right flat hand.
THE (definite article): Twist the right *T* hand to the right from a palm-left position.
THERE: Point with the right index finger to an imaginary object.
WHERE: Shake the right

index finger back and forth, palm forward.

planes (trains)? Follow me.

Go together (yourself). Have

a good trip. Take

FOLLOW, CHASE: Hold the *A* hands to the front, right behind left, and move both hands forward together. Sign *chase* more rapidly.
GO: Circle the index fingers around each other as they move forward.
GOOD, WELL: Touch the lips with the right flat hand. Bring the right hand down into the left hand, palms up.
HAVE, HAD, HAS, OWN, POSSESS: Move the bent-hands fingertips to the chest.

ME: Point to or touch the chest with the right index finger.
PLANE, AIRPLANE, FLY, JET: Move the right *Y* hand, with index finger extended, in the air.
TAKE: Move the right open hand from right to left, ending with a closed hand near the body.
TOGETHER, ACCOMPA-NY: Hold the *A* hands together, palms facing, and circle them from right to left.

TRAIN, RAILROAD: Rub the right *H* fingers over the left *H* fingers, palms down, several times.
TRIP, JOURNEY, TRAVEL: Move the curved right *V* hand in a forward wavy movement, palm down.
YOURSELF, HERSELF, HIMSELF, ITSELF, THEM-SELVES: Push the right *A* hand forward, thumb up, in several short movements toward a person or object.

a   taxi.   My   car

   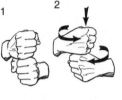

(flat tire)   is   being   fixed.

What   do   the   tickets   cost?

BEING: Place the right *B* hand at the mouth and move it forward.
CAR, DRIVE: Make two *S* hands. Pretend to be steering a car.
COST, CHARGE, FINE, PRICE, TAX: Hit the right bent index finger across and down the left palm.
DO, ACTION, DID, DONE: Move both *C* hands, palms down, in unison to the left, then to the right.
FIX, MAKE: Hit the left *S*

hand with the right *S* hand. Twist the hands in. Then repeat.
FLAT TIRE, DEFLATE: Place the right open *and*-hand thumb on the left flat palm and close the right hand to an *and* hand.
IS: Place the right *I* hand at the mouth. Move it forward.
MY, MINE, OWN: Place the right flat hand on the chest.
TAXI: Make two *T* hands. Pretend to be steering a car.

THE (definite article): Twist the right *T* hand to the right from a palm-left position.
TICKET: Grasp the lower portion of the left palm between the right curved *V* fingers.
WHAT: Move the tip of the right index finger across the left flat palm.

 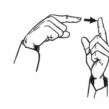 

The   trip   to   Europe

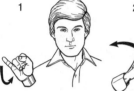   

(Jerusalem)   last year   was

exciting.   How   far   is

EUROPE, EUROPEAN: Move the right *E* hand in a small circle at the right side of the head, palm out. When referring to a *European* person, add *person ending*.
EXCITING, EXCITE: Brush the middle fingers on the chest with forward circular movements several times with other fingers extended.
FAR, DISTANT, REMOTE: Place the *A* hands together, palms facing, and move the right hand forward.

HOW: Place both bent hands together back to back. Turn them forward until the hands are flat, palms up.
IS: *(See page 118.)*
JERUSALEM: Sign *J* with right hand. Then, touch both flat-hand fingertips together forming a triangle. Repeat a couple of times as hands move to the right.
LAST YEAR: Rotate the right *S* hand around the left *S* hand, ending with the

right hand on the left. Next, move the right hand up and back until the index points over the right shoulder.
TO: Touch the left vertical index fingertip with the right index fingertip.
TRIP, JOURNEY, TRAVEL: Move the right curved *V* hand in a forward wavy movement, palm down.
WAS: Move the right *W* hand backward near the right cheek and close it to an *S* hand.

the   highway   (bridge)?   The

car   won't   start.   I

got   a   parking   ticket.

A: Move the right *A*-hand in a small arc to the right.
BRIDGE: Touch the right *V*-hand fingertips under the left wrist and then under the left arm near the elbow.
CAR, DRIVE: Make two *S* hands. Pretend to be steering a car.
GOT, GET: Move the open hands together in front of the body with the right hand on top of the left, forming *S* hands.
HIGHWAY, STREET,

AVENUE, PATH, ROAD, WAY: Face both flat hands palm to palm and move them forward in a winding movement.
I: Place the right *I* hand on the chest, palm left.
PARK (a vehicle): Place the right *3* hand on top of the left flat palm with fingers pointing forward.
START, BEGIN: Twist the right *one* hand index finger in the *V* shape of the flat left hand.

THE (definite article): Twist the right *T* hand to the right from a palm-left position.
TICKET: Grasp the lower portion of the left palm between the right curved *V* fingers.
WON'T, REFUSE: Move the right *S* (or *A*) hand quickly back over the right shoulder as the head is turned left.

How much is a

 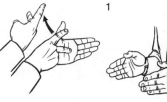 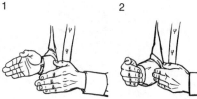

single (double) room?

What hotel are you

ARE: Move the right *R* hand forward from the lips.
DOUBLE, TWICE: Place the right *2* middle finger in the left palm and flip it up. *Double* can be signed with *D* hand.
HOTEL: Place the right *H* hand on the left index finger, which is pointing up. Move the *H* fingers forward and back.
HOW: Place both bent hands together back to back. Turn them forward until the hands are flat, palms up.
IS: Place the right *I* hand at the mouth and move it forward.
MUCH, LOT: With palms facing, hold the open, slightly curved hands in front and move them apart.
ROOM: With palms facing, hold the flat hands to the front. Then move the hands, placing the left behind the right and parallel. The *R* hands can be used.
SINGLE: Circle the right vertical index finger, palm in.
WHAT: Move the tip of the right index finger across the left flat palm.
YOU: Point to the person you are signing to. Move the right hand from left to right if there is more than one person.

 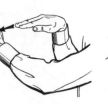  

staying   at?   What   country
national territory

(state)   is   D a n   from?

He   rides   a

A: Move the right *A* hand in a small arc to the right.

AT: Touch the right flat-hand fingertips against the back of the left flat hand, or fingerspell it.

COUNTRY (national territory): Rub the right *Y* hand, palm in, in a circle near the left elbow.

FROM: Touch the right *X* index finger on the left vertical index finger and move it back and away.

HE, HIM: Pretend to be gripping a cap with the right hand. Move it forward a little. Then point the index forward. If the gender is obvious, omit gripping a cap.

IS: Place the right *I* hand at the mouth and move it forward.

RIDE (in a vehicle): Make an *O* with the left hand. Place the right curved *U* fingers into it. Move both hands forward.

STATE (geographical): Move the right *S* hand down the left flat hand from fingers to palm.

STAY, REMAIN: Place the right *A* thumb tip on left *A* thumb tip. Push them down together.

WHAT: Move the tip of the right index finger across the left flat palm.

motorcycle.   Climb   up   (down).

  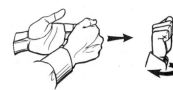

Get in.   Get out.   Lead   the

way.   Wait   on   the

CLIMB: With curved *V* hands facing, make a climbing motion, one hand over the other.

DOWN: Point down with the right index finger; move hand down a little.

GET IN: Place the right curved *V* fingers into the left *O* hand.

GET OUT: Take the right curved *V* fingers out of the left *O* hand.

LEAD, CONDUCT, GUIDE: Grasp the fingers of the left flat hand and pull them forward.

MOTORCYCLE: Place the *S* hands apart, palms down, and to the front. Pivot both hands forward and backward using the wrists.

ON: Place the right flat hand on top of the left flat hand, palms down.

THE (definite article): Twist the right *T* hand to the right from a palm-left position.

UP: Point up with the right index finger and move hand up a little.

WAIT, PENDING: Face both curved open hands to the left, palms up, right behind left, and wiggle the fingers.

WAY, AVENUE, HIGHWAY, PATH, ROAD, STREET: Face both flat hands palm to palm and move them forward in a winding movement.

corner. Don't wander. Cross

here. Where are you

going? I need directions.

ARE: Move the right *R* hand forward from the lips.
CORNER: Touch both flat-hand fingertips at a 90° (or right) angle. Some use index fingers only.
CROSS, ACROSS, OVER: Slide the right flat hand (little-finger edge) over back of left flat hand, palm down.
DIRECTION: Shake the right *D* hand back and forth.
DON'T, DOESN'T, DO NOT, NOT: Put the right *A*-hand thumb under the chin. Move it quickly forward.
GO: Circle the index fingers around each other as they move forward.
HERE: Move both flat hands, palms up, in opposite forward circles in front of the body.
I: Place the right *I* hand on the chest, palm left.
NEED, HAVE TO, MUST, NECESSARY, SHOULD: Move the right bent index finger down forcefully several times.

WANDER, STRAY: Place both index fingers side by side, palms down and pointing forward. Move the right hand forward and to the right.
WHERE: Shake the right index finger back and forth.
YOU: Point to the person you are signing to. Move the right hand from left to right if there is more than one person.

Go   the   opposite   way.

Parallel   park.   Turn   right.

Move   toward   the   left.

GO: Circle the index fingers around each other as they move forward.
LEFT (direction): Move the right *L* hand to the left with palm forward.
MOVE, PUT: Hold the open curved hands to the left front, palms down. Move them together up and down to the right while closing them to *and* hands.
OPPOSITE: Hold the index fingertips (or *O* hands) together and move them apart in opposite directions.
PARALLEL: With palms down, move both extended index fingers forward together. Fingers do not touch.
PARK (a vehicle): Place the right *3* hand on top of the left flat palm with fingers pointing forward.
RIGHT (direction): Move the right *R* hand, palm forward, to the right.
THE (definite article): Twist the right *T* hand to the right from a palm-left position.
TOWARD: Move the right index finger toward the left vertical index finger. Fingers do not touch.
TURN: Rotate the index fingers in right-to-left circles around each other with the right pointing down and left pointing up.
WAY, AVENUE, HIGHWAY, PATH, ROAD, STREET: Face both flat hands palm to palm and move them forward in a winding movement.

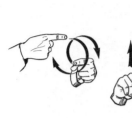   

Go   north   (south)   (east)

(west).   I   know   the   way.

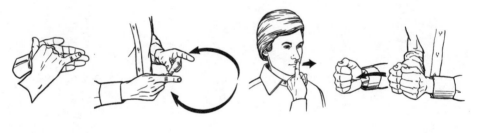

That   place   is   far.

EAST: With palm forward, move right *E* hand to right.
FAR, DISTANT, REMOTE: Place the *A* hands together, palms facing, and move the right hand forward.
GO: Circle the index fingers as they move forward.
I: Place the right *I* hand on the chest, palm left.
IS: Place right *I* hand at the mouth and move it forward.
KNOW, INTELLIGENCE, KNOWLEDGE, RECOGNIZE: Touch the fingertips

of the right hand on the forehead several times.
NORTH: Move right *N* hand up.
PLACE, AREA, LOCATION: Touch the *P*-hand fingers, palms facing, to the front and move them back in opposite semicircles, touching fingers again near the body. *Area, location,* and *place* may be initialized.
SOUTH: With palm forward, move right *S* hand down.
THAT: Place the right *Y*

hand in the left flat palm.
WAY, AVENUE, HIGHWAY, PATH, ROAD, STREET: Face both flat hands palm to palm and move them forward in a winding movement.
WE, US: Touch the right shoulder with the right index finger. Then, circle it forward and back until it touches the left shoulder. The *W* can be used for *we* and *U* for *us*.
WEST: With palm forward, move the right *W* hand to left.

We   visited   <u>Canada.</u>   Mexico.

Use any of the following signs.

England.   Israel.   Germany.   Spain.

Africa.   Russia.   Japan.   China.

AFRICA, AFRICAN: Make a circle with right *A* hand in front of face. Add *person ending* for *African* person.
CANADA, CANADIAN: Grasp and shake right side of shirt with right hand. Add *person ending* for *Canadian* person.
CHINA, CHINESE: Touch left then right chest with right index finger. Bring right index down. Add *person ending* for *Chinese* person.
ENGLAND, ENGLISH: Hold left hand wrist with right

curved hand; move them forward and back. For *English,* add *person ending.*
GERMANY, GERMAN: Cross hands at wrists with palms facing body and wiggle the fingers. Add *person ending* for *German* person.
ISRAEL, ISRAELI: Slide the right *I* finger down each side of the chin. Add *person ending* for *Israeli* person.
JAPAN, JAPANESE: Point extended fingers of both *G* hands at each other; pull

them to sides while closing *G* hands. Add *person ending* for *Japanese* person.
MEXICO, MEXICAN: Slide right *M*-hand fingertips down right cheek a few times. Add *person ending* for *Mexican* person.
RUSSIA, RUSSIAN: Tap open hands on waist a few times. Add *person ending* for *Russian* person.
SPAIN: *(See page 128.)*
VISIT: *(See page 133.)*
WE: *(See page 126.)*

I'm   going   to

California. Chicago. Los Angeles. Boston.
Use any of the following signs.

Ohio.   Florida.   New York. Arizona.

AM: Move the right *A*-hand thumb forward from the lips.
ARIZONA: With palm facing left, slide the right *A*-hand thumb across the chin from right to left.
BOSTON: Move the right *B* hand down near the right shoulder, palm forward.
CALIFORNIA: Touch the right ear with the right index finger. Bring the *Y* hand forward and shake it. (*California* and *gold* are the same sign.)
CHICAGO: Move right *C*

hand to the right and down.
FLORIDA: Fingerspell *F* and *L* with right hand.
GO: Circle the index fingers around each other as they move forward.
I: Place the right *I* hand on the chest, palm left.
LOS ANGELES: Fingerspell *L* and *A* with right hand.
NEW YORK: Slide the right *Y* hand back and forth on the left flat hand.
OHIO: Fingerspell *O* and *H*

with right hand.
SPAIN, SPANISH: Touch the shoulders with the index fingers. Then, interlock the fingers. Add the *person ending* sign when referring to a *Spanish* person.
TO: Touch the left vertical index fingertip with the right index fingertip.

Time, Weather, and Holidays

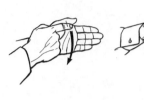  

What time is it?

We usually leave early

in the morning. They

EARLY: Slide the right curved middle finger over the back of the left closed hand.

IN: Place right *and*-hand fingertips into the left *C* hand.

IS: Place right *I* hand at the mouth and move it forward.

IT: Touch the right *I* finger in the flat left palm.

LEAVE, DEPART, RETIRE: Hold both flat hands to the right, palms down, and draw them up to self, ending in *A* hands.

MORNING: Bend left arm and rest left hand in the bend of right arm. Hold right hand flat and arm bent horizontally. Move the right arm upright, palm facing self.

THEY, THEM, THESE, THOSE: Point forward or to the people or objects with the right index finger and move the hand to the right.

TIME, CLOCK, WATCH: Tap the left wrist a few times with the right curved index finger.

WE, US: Touch the right shoulder with the right index finger. Then, circle it forward and back until it touches the left shoulder. The *W* can be used for *we* and *U* for *us*.

USUALLY, USED TO: Rest the *U*-hand wrist on the palm-down closed hand wrist. Move both hands down a little.

WHAT: Move the tip of the right index finger across the left flat palm.

go   there   often   (sometimes).

   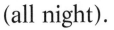 

Mom   stayed   all day   (all night).

Did   you   wait   long?

ALL DAY: Hold left arm flat, index finger pointing right. Place elbow of bent right arm on left index finger. Start with index finger far to the right and move right arm across the body in a full arc resting on the left arm.

ALL NIGHT, OVERNIGHT: Place the left arm horizontal in front of the body, with flat hand palm down and finger-tips touching crook of right arm. Hold the right curved hand forward and move it in a downward arc until it rests under the left arm.

DID: *(See page 137.)*
GO: *(See page 137.)*
LONG: Move the right index finger up the left arm.
MOM, MOTHER: Touch the thumb of the right open hand against the chin.
OFTEN, FREQUENT: Arc the upturned right bent hand into the flat left palm a few times.
SOMETIMES: Place right index finger in left flat palm, which faces right. Move the index finger up and vertical. Pause and repeat action.

STAY, REMAIN: Place the right *A* thumb tip on left *A* thumb tip. Push them down together.
THERE: Point with the right index finger to an imaginary object.
WAIT, PENDING: Face both curved open hands to the left, palms up, right behind left, and wiggle the fingers.
YOU: *(See page 137.)*

Five   minutes.   Wait   a   moment.

 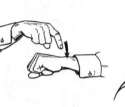 

My   watch   is   wrong.

Come   this   afternoon (evening).

AFTERNOON: Hold the right forearm at a 45-degree angle on the back of the left flat hand, which is horizontal and palm down.

COME: Circle the index fingers as they move toward the body.

EVENING, NIGHT: Place the right curved hand over the flat horizontal left hand.

FIVE: Hold up right open hand with palm forward.

IS: Place the right *I* hand at mouth and move it forward.

MINUTE: Place the right *1*-hand index finger against the vertical left flat palm, which faces right. Move the right index finger past the left little finger.

MOMENT, SECOND (time): Place the right *1* hand against the vertical flat left hand. Move index finger forward a little in a short arc.

MY, MINE, OWN: Place the right flat hand on the chest.

THIS: Move both *Y* (or flat) hands down, palms up, at the same time for something abstract.

WAIT, PENDING: Face both curved open hands to the left, palms up, right behind left, and wiggle the fingers.

WATCH, TIME, CLOCK: Tap the left wrist a few times with the right curved index finger.

WRONG, ERROR, MISTAKE: Hold the right *Y* hand on the chin, palm in.

I   am   going   home

next year.   Someday   we   will

visit.   What   time   will

AM: Move the right *A*-hand thumb forward from the lips.
GO: Circle the index fingers around each other as they move forward.
HOME: Touch the right *and*-hand fingertips on the mouth then on the right cheek.
I: Place the right *I* hand on the chest, palm left.
NEXT YEAR, YEAR: Rotate the right *S* hand around the left *S* hand, ending with right hand on left. Point forward with the right index finger. Do not point forward for *year.*
SOMEDAY, FUTURE: Move the right flat hand forward in an arc from the right side of the head. To indicate a distant future, make a larger arc.
TIME, CLOCK, WATCH: Tap the left wrist a few times with the right curved index finger.
VISIT: Place both *V* hands up, palms in, and move them in alternating forward circles.
WE, US: Touch the right shoulder with the right index finger. Then, circle it forward and back until it touches the left shoulder. The *W* can be used for *we* and *U* for *us.*
WHAT: Move the tip of the right index finger across the left flat palm.
WILL (verb), SHALL, WOULD: Hold the right flat hand to the right side of the face and move it forward.

D   a   v   e   arrive?   I

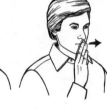

will   be   there   next

month.   That   happened   ages

AGE, ERA, TIMES, TIME (abstract): Circle the right *T* hand on the vertical left flat palm.

ARRIVE, GET TO, REACH: Move the right curved hand forward into the palm of the left curved hand, palms face self.

BE: Place the right *B* hand at the mouth and move it forward.

HAPPEN, EVENT, OCCUR: Hold both index fingers up and to the front with palms facing. Simultaneously pivot both hands to a palm-forward position.

I: Place the right *I* hand on the chest, palm left.

MONTH, MONTHLY: Move the horizontal right index finger down the vertical left index finger. For *monthly*, repeat several times

NEXT: Place flat hands to front, palms in, right behind left. Place the right hand over and ahead of the left.

THAT: Place the right *Y* hand in the left flat palm.

THERE: Point with the right index finger to an imaginary object.

WILL (verb), SHALL, WOULD: Hold the right flat hand to the right side of the face and move it forward.

ago. Not yet. Please wait

until noon. Be home

b y midnight. Meet me

AGO, LAST, PAST, PREVIOUSLY, USED TO: With palm facing body, move right flat hand backward over right shoulder. Making the sign more slowly and larger indicates a greater length of time.

BE: (See page 134.)

HOME: Touch the right and-hand fingertips on the mouth, then on the right cheek.

NOT YET, LATE: Move right flat hand back and forth a few times near right side.

ME: Point to or touch the chest with the right index finger.

MEET, ENCOUNTER: Extend the index fingers of both hands and hold them at the sides with palms facing. Bring both hands together.

MIDNIGHT: Slide the edge of the right flat hand across and over the back of the horizontal flat left hand.

NOON: Bend the left arm and hold the left flat hand horizontal. Place the bent vertical right arm elbow on fingertips of the left hand.

PLEASE, ENJOY, LIKE, PLEASURE: Put the right hand over the heart and move it in a small circle.

UNTIL: Touch the right index finger, palm out, to the tip of the left index finger, palm in, in a forward arc.

WAIT, PENDING: Face both curved open hands to the left, palms up, right behind left, and wiggle the fingers.

before   (after)   9   A.   M.

They   came   yesterday   (recently).

We   are   next.   Can

AFTER (time): Move the slightly curved right hand forward and away from the sightly curved left hand.
ARE: *(See page 137.)*
BEFORE (time): Hold both slightly curved hands to the front near each other, right behind left. Move the right hand backward.
CAME, COME: Circle the index fingers as they move toward the body.
CAN, ABILITY, ABLE, COMPETENT, COULD,

POSSIBLE: Move both *S* (or *A*) hands down together.
IS: *(See page 137.)*
NEXT: Place flat hands to front, palms in, right behind left. Place the right hand over and ahead of the left.
NINE: Touch right thumb with the index finger, other fingers extended, palm forward.
RECENTLY: Move the curved right index finger up and down a couple of times as it rests against the right cheek, palm facing back.

THEY, THEM, THESE, THOSE: Point forward or to the people or objects with the right index finger and move the hand to the right.
WE, US: Touch the right shoulder with the right index finger. Then, circle it forward and back until it touches the left shoulder. The *W* can be used for *we* and *U* for *us*.
YESTERDAY: Place the right *Y* (or *A*)-hand thumb on the right chin. Move it back toward ear in an arc.

you

go

later?

When

does

school

start?

Next

week.

The

weather

is

ARE: Move the right *R* hand forward from the lips.
DOES, DO, DID, ACTION, DONE: Move both *C* hands, palms down, in unison to the left, then to the right.
GO: Circle the index fingers around each other as they move forward.
IS: Place the right *I* hand at the mouth and move it forward.
LATER, AFTERWARD: Hold the right *L* hand in the vertical left palm and twist it

forward and down.
NEXT: Place flat hands to front, palms in, right behind left. Place the right hand over and ahead of the left.
SCHOOL: Clap the hands two times.
START, BEGIN: Twist the right *one*-hand index finger in the *V* shape of the flat left hand.
WEATHER: Face both *W* hands and twist them up and down.
WEEK: Slide the right index

finger forward over the left flat palm.
WHEN: Move the right index finger around the left upright index finger. Then touch the tip of the right index finger on the tip of the left index finger.
YOU: Point to the person you are signing to. Move the right hand from left to right if there is more than one person.

  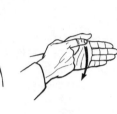 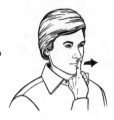

perfect   (bad).   What   is

the   temperature?   Is   it

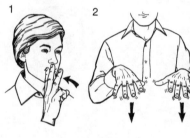 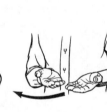 

raining?   Bring   your

BAD: Touch the lips with the fingertips of the right flat hand. Then turn the hand and move it down with the palm facing down.
BRING: Move both open hands either toward self, another person, or in the direction needed, palms up, with one hand a little ahead of the other.
IS: Place the right *I* hand at mouth and move it forward.
IT: Touch the right *I* finger in the flat left palm.

PERFECT: Touch both *P* hand middle fingers together.
RAIN: Sign *water* by touching the right side of the mouth a couple of times with the right *W* index finger. Then wiggle the fingers of both hands as they move down. Some omit the sign for *water*.
TEMPERATURE, FEVER, THERMOMETER: Slide the right index finger up and down the left vertical index finger.

WHAT: Move the tip of the right index finger across the left flat palm.
YOUR, YOURS, HIS, HER, THEIR: Push the right flat palm forward toward the person being spoken to. If it is not clear from the context, the *male* or *female* sign can be used first. When using *your* in the plural, push the right flat palm forward, then move it to the right.

umbrella.   Today   is

hot   (cold).   Yesterday   it

snowed.   The   road

COLD, CHILLY, WINTER: Shake the upheld *S* hands in front of the chest.

HOT, HEAT: Hold the right *C* hand at the mouth and quickly turn it forward to the right.

IS: Place the right *I* hand at the mouth and move it forward.

IT: Touch the right *I* finger in the flat left palm.

ROAD, STREET, AVENUE, HIGHWAY, PATH, WAY: Face both flat hands palm to palm and move them forward in a winding movement.

SNOW: Place the right curved open hand on chest. Move it forward to an *and* hand. Next move the open hands down as the fingers wiggle.

THE (definite article): Twist the right *T* hand to the right from a palm-left position.

TODAY: Move both *Y* (or flat) hands down, palms up, at the same time. Hold left arm flat, index finger pointing right. Place the elbow of the bent right arm on the left index finger. Move the right arm, index finger up, across the body in a short arc.

UMBRELLA: Place the right *S* hand over the left *S* hand and move the right hand up a little.

YESTERDAY: Place the right *Y* (or *A*)-hand thumb on the right chin. Move it back toward the ear in an arc.

is   covered   with   ice.

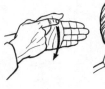   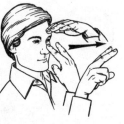

What   is   the   weather   forecast?

Mostly   sunshine.   Last   month

COVER: Move the curved right hand over the curved left hand, palms down.
FORECAST, PROPHECY, VISION: Point the right *V* fingertips toward the eyes. Twist the hand and move it forward under the left flat hand.
ICE, FREEZE: Drop the open hands down, stopping with all fingers bent rigidly, palms down.
IS: Place the right *I* hand at the mouth and move it forward.

LAST, FINAL, END: Strike the left little finger with the right index finger. Both little fingers can be used.
MONTH, MONTHLY: Move the horizontal right index finger down the vertical left index finger. For *monthly*, repeat several times
MOSTLY, MOST: Bring the right *and* hand up to meet the left *and* hand, fingertips touching. Then move the right *A* hand up.
SUNSHINE: Make a left-to-

right circle above the head with the right index finger pointing forward. Then move the *and* hand across the chest downward, ending with an open hand.
WEATHER: Face both *W* hands and twist them up and down.
WHAT: Move the tip of the right index finger across the left flat palm.
WITH: Place both *A* hands together, palms facing.

was	warm	(cool).	There

is	a	drought.	Look

at	the	beautiful	sunset

AT: Touch the right flat-hand fingertips against the back of the left flat hand, or fingerspell it.
BEAUTIFUL, PRETTY: Place the fingertips of the right *and* hand on the chin. Open hand as it circles the face from right to left. End with *and* hand near chin.
COOL: Bend and unbend the flat (or open) hands at the front sides of the face with palms in.
DROUGHT, DRY: Slide the curved right index from left to right across the mouth.
IS: Place the right *I* hand at the mouth. Move it forward.
LOOK, LOOK AT, LOOK AT ME, LOOK BACK, LOOK DOWN, OBSERVE, WATCH: Point the right *V* hand to the eyes. Twist the *V* hand and point it forward. For *look at me*, *look back*, and *look down*, point the right *V* hand at the eyes, then in the direction needed.
SUNSET: Hold the left flat hand and arm horizontal, palm down. Place the right *O* hand in front of and above the left arm and move it in an arc below the left arm.
THERE: Point the right index finger to an imaginary object.
WARM: Place the right *A* hand at the mouth, palm in, and open the hand slowly as it moves forward and up.
WAS: Move the right *W* hand backward near the right cheek and close it to an *S* hand.

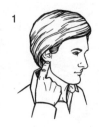

(sunrise).   The   thunder

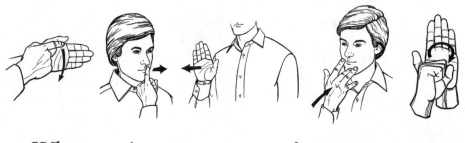

(lightning)   storm   has   ended.

What   is   your   favorite season?

END, COMPLETE, DONE, FINISH: Slide the flat right hand off the edge of the left flat hand and down.
FAVORITE: Touch the chin several times with the right middle finger.
HAS, HAVE, HAD, OWN, POSSESS: Move the bent-hands fingertips to chest.
IS: *(See page 141.)*
LIGHTNING: Quickly draw a jagged line in the air with the right index finger.

hand in a circle on left palm.
STORM, CLOUD: Place the open hands, palms facing, to the front at head level. Make circular up and down move-ments as hands move to other side. Make movements less vigorous for *cloud.*
SUNRISE: Hold the left flat hand and arm horizontal, palm down. Place right *O* hand in front of and below the left arm and move it in an arc above the left arm.
THUNDER: Point to the right

ear with the right index fin-ger. Move both closed hands, palms down, alternately back and forth a few times.
WHAT: *(See page 143.)*
YOUR, YOURS, HIS, HER, THEIR: Push the right flat palm forward toward the per-son being spoken to. If it is not clear from the context, the *male* or *female* sign can be used first. When using *your* in the plural, push the right flat palm forward, then move it to the right.

Spring,   Summer,   Winter,   or

Fall?   Can   you   come
Autumn

to   the   party?   The   parade

CAN, ABILITY, ABLE, COMPETENT, COULD, POSSIBLE: Move both *S* (or *A*) hands down together.
COME: Circle the index fingers as they move toward the body.
FALL, AUTUMN: Slide the right flat-hand index finger down the left forearm, which is held in front at an angle.
OR, EITHER: Touch the left *L*-hand thumb and index finger several times with the right index finger.

PARADE: Place the bent left open hand in front of the right bent open hand. Swing them from side to side as both hands move forward.
PARTY: Swing the *P* hands left and right with palms down.
SPRING, GROW, MATURE: Pass the right *and* hand up and through the left *C* hand while opening the fingers.
SUMMER: Wipe the curved right index finger, from left to right, across forehead.

TO: Touch the left vertical index fingertip with the right index fingertip.
WHAT: Move the tip of right index finger across left flat palm.
WINTER, COLD, CHILLY: Shake the upheld *S* hands in front of the chest.
YOU: Point to the person you are signing to. Move the right hand from left to right if there is more than one person.

 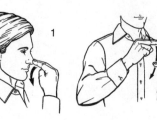 

was	fun	(lousy).

Thanks	for	the	gift.

Surprise	her	with	flowers.

FLOWER: Move the fingertips of the right *and* hand under one nostril then the other.

FOR: Place the right index finger at the right temple. Twist it forward as the hand moves forward.

FUN: Brush the nose with the right *U* fingers. Then brush the left and right *U* fingers against each other several times.

GIFT, REWARD: Hold the modified *A* hands in front, palms facing; move them forward together in an arc.

HER, SHE: Trace the jaw with the right *A*-hand thumb. Then point forward. If the gender is obvious, omit tracing the jaw.

LOUSY, ROTTEN: Place the right *3*-hand thumb on the nose and quickly move it downward in an arc.

SURPRISE, ASTONISH: Hold the closed hands at the sides of the face and flick both index fingers up at the same time.

THANKS, THANK YOU, YOU'RE WELCOME: Smile and bring the fingertips of both flat hands to the lips. Move the hands forward until palms are up. One hand can be used.

WAS: Move the right *W* hand backward near the right cheek and close it to an *S* hand.

WITH: Place both *A* hands together, palms facing.

Have a happy <u>holiday</u>. Hanukkah.

Use any of the following signs.

Birthday. Thanksgiving.

Valentine's. Easter. Christmas. New Year.

BIRTHDAY: With palms up, hold right hand in left hand and move them forward and up. Bend left arm, pointing index finger right. Bend and rest right elbow on left index finger with right index finger pointing up. Move right arm in a short arc across chest.
CHRISTMAS: Move the right *C* hand from left to right in a small arc.
EASTER: With palm forward, move the right *E* hand in a small arc to the right.

HANUKKAH: Point *H* hands palms down; swing them up to *4* hands, palms in.
HAPPY, GLAD, JOY: Move flat hands (or one) in forward circles, fingers touch chest alternately (or unison.)
HAVE, HAD, HAS, OWN, POSSESS: *(See page 150.)*
HOLIDAY, VACATION, LEISURE: Place thumbs at armpits and wiggle fingers.
NEW YEAR: Brush the slightly curved right hand across and over the palm of

the left hand. Then rotate the right *S* hand around the left *S* hand, ending with right hand on the left.
THANKSGIVING: Bring fingertips of both (or one) flat hands to lips. Move hands forward until palms are up. Place *and* hands in front, palms down; move them forward, changing to palms-up flat hands.
VALENTINE: Draw a heart shape over heart with *V* hands.

It   is   Sunday.   Monday.

Use any of the following signs.

Tuesday.   Wednesday.   Thursday.   Friday.

Saturday.   cloudy.   windy.   dark.

CLOUD, STORM: Place the open hands, palms facing, to the front at head level. Make circular up-and-down movements as the hands move to the other side. Make movements more vigorous for *storm*.

DARK, DIM: Move the flat palms down as they cross in front of the face, palms in.

FRIDAY: Move the right *F* hand in a small circle.

IS: Place right *I* hand at the mouth and move it forward.

IT: Touch the right *I* finger in the flat left palm.

MONDAY: Move the right *M* hand in a small circle.

SATURDAY: Move the right *S* hand in a small circle.

SUNDAY: Move both flat hands together in opposite circles to the front with palms forward. Circles can go left or right.

THURSDAY: Move the right *H* hand in a small circle. Sometimes signed with a *T* and *H*.

TUESDAY: Move the right *T* hand in a small circle.

WEDNESDAY: Move the right *W* hand in a small circle.

WIND, BREEZE: Sweep both open hands palm to palm, back and forth together from left to right several times at head level.

Animals, Nature, and Science

Do   you   have   animals?

Cat   or   dog?   We

feed   the   birds   (squirrels).

ANIMAL: With fingertips on the chest, rock both bent hands in and out sideways.
BIRD: Hold the right *Q* hand at the side of the mouth. Open and close the index finger and thumb a few times.
CAT: Place the thumbs and index fingers of both *F* hands under the nose. Move them sideways.
DO, DID, ACTION, DONE: Move both *C* hands, palms down, in unison to the left, then to the right.
DOG: Slap the right hand on the right leg and snap the fingers.
FEED, EAT: Move the fingertips of the right *and* hand to the mouth a few times.
HAVE, HAD, HAS, OWN, POSSESS: Move the bent-hands fingertips to the chest.
OR, EITHER: Touch the left *L*-hand thumb and index finger several times with the right index finger.

SQUIRREL: Place the bent *V* fingers with palms facing. Hit the fingers together several times.
WE, US: Touch the right shoulder with the right index finger. Then, circle it forward and back until it touches the left shoulder. The *W* can be used for *we* and *U* for *us*.
YOU: Point to the person you are signing to. Move the right hand from left to right if there is more than one person.

My

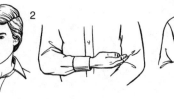

son

likes

dinosaurs

(kangaroos).

She

is   afraid   o f   spiders,

AFRAID, SCARED: Thrust the *and* hands simultaneously in front of the chest from the sides as they change to open hands.

DINOSAUR: Point the left flat hand to the right with palm facing down. Rest the right elbow on the back of the left hand with the right arm held up. Move the right bent *and* hand back and forth a few times.

IS: Place the right *I* hand at mouth and move it forward.

KANGAROO: Move the right bent hand forward in a double arc movement. Two hands can be used.

LIKE, ADMIRE: Hold the thumb and index finger of the right open hand on the chest. Move the hand forward, closing the thumb and index finger.

MY, MINE, OWN: Place the right flat hand on the chest.

SHE, HER: Trace the jaw with the right *A*-hand thumb. Then point forward. If the

gender is obvious, omit tracing the jaw.

SON: Pretend to grip a cap and move the right hand forward a little. Place the right flat hand, palm up, in the crook of the bent left arm.

SPIDER: Cross the curved open hands, palms down, and interlock the fingers. Wiggle the fingers as the hands move forward.

bugs, and mice. Look

at the fountain (horse) (skunk)

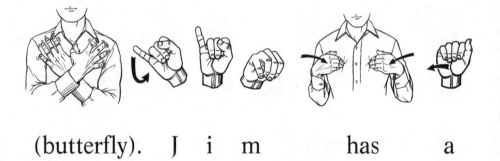

(butterfly). J i m has a

....

AND: *(See page 151.)*
AT: Touch the right flat-hand fingertips against the back of the left flat hand, or fingerspell it.
BUG, INSECT: Place the thumb of the right *3* hand on the nose. Move the index finger and middle finger up and down several times.
BUTTERFLY: Cross both open hands in front of the chest and interlock the thumbs. Wiggle the fingers and wave the hands.

FOUNTAIN, SPRING: Pass the right *and* hand up and through the left *C* hand. Wiggle the fingers as the right fingers appear on top, over, and down the outside of the *C* hand.
HAS, HAVE, HAD, OWN, POSSESS: Move the bent-hands fingertips to chest.
HORSE: Place the thumb of the right *U* hand on the right temple and bend *U* fingers up and down several times.
LOOK, LOOK AT, LOOK

AT ME, LOOK BACK, LOOK DOWN, OBSERVE, WATCH: Point the right *V* hand to the eyes. Twist the *V* hand and point it forward. For *look at me, look back,* and *look down,* point the right *V* hand at the eyes, then in the direction needed.
MICE, MOUSE: Move the right index finger across the nose several times.
SKUNK: Move right *K* hand backward over the head.

farm   with   cows,   pigs,

and   sheep.   Dad   went

   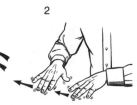

fishing   at   the   river.

AND: Move the right open hand to the right as the hand closes to all fingertips touching.

AT: Touch the right flat-hand fingertips against the back of the left flat hand, or fingerspell it.

COW: Hold both *Y*-hand thumbs at the temples and twist up until little fingers point up. This sign can be made using only the right hand.

DAD, FATHER: Touch the thumb of the right open hand on the forehead.

FARM, COUNTRY (rural): Move the right open-hand thumb from left to right across the chin.

FISHING: Pretend to be holding a fishing rod with both *A* hands and move it backward and forward.

PIG: Bend and unbend the right flat hand under the chin a few times.

RIVER: Place the right *W* hand at the side of the mouth several times. Move the open hands to the left or right as the fingers wiggle.

SHEEP: Open and close the right *V* fingers as they move up the left arm.

WENT, GO: Circle the index fingers around each other as they move forward.

WITH: Place both *A* hands together, palms facing.

Kill   the   fly.   The

sky   is   full   o f

stars   tonight.   The   moon

FLY (insect): Sweep the right curved hand across the top of the left closed hand and forearm, ending with the right hand closed.
FULL, FILLED: Pass the right flat hand to the left over the index side of the closed left hand.
IS: Place the right *I* hand at mouth and move it forward.
KILL: Push the right index finger under the palm-down curved left hand, and twist it to the right.

MOON: Place the right *C* hand over the right eye.
SKY, HEAVENS, SPACE: Move the right flat hand above the head in an arc from left to right.
STAR: Alternately strike glancing blows off the sides of both index fingers as they move upward from in front of the face.
TONIGHT: Sign *this* and *night*. Move both *Y* (or flat) hands down, palms up, at the same time. Place the

right curved hand over the left horizontal flat hand and point down.

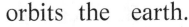

orbits   the   earth.   This   field

(valley)   has   good   soil.

   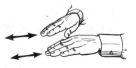

I   love   nature   walks.

EARTH: Hold left closed hand between the right index and thumb and rock right hand from left to right.
GOOD, WELL: Touch the lips with right flat hand. Bring the right hand down into left hand, palms up.
HAS, HAVE, HAD, OWN, POSSESS: Move the bent-hands fingertips to chest.
I: Place the right *I* hand on the chest, palm left.
FIELD, LAND: Rub the *and*-hand fingertips and thumbs

together, palms up. Circle flat hands in opposite directions to front, palms down.
LOVE: Cross the *S* hands at the wrists over the heart.
NATURE, NATURAL: Move the right *N* hand in a circle over the left flat hand. Then rest the right *N* fingers on the back of left flat hand.
ORBIT: Move the right index in a forward circle around left *S* hand, then place it on the left *S* hand.
SOIL, DIRT, GROUND: Rub

fingertips and thumbs of both curved hands in front of the body with palms facing up.
THIS: Place the right index in the left flat palm.
VALLEY: Hold both flat hands up with palms down and to the sides. Move them in a slight wavy motion until they meet in front of waist.
WALK, STEP: Imitate walking by placing both hands palms down and alternately moving each hand forward.

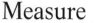   

Measure the wood. Be creative.

  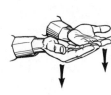 

That is heavy (light).

    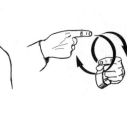

Should we go rock

BE: Place the right *B* hand at the mouth and move it forward.
CREATIVE, CREATE, INVENT: Push the right *4-* hand index finger, palm left, up the center of the fore-head the full length of the index finger.
GO: Circle the index fingers around each other as they move forward.
HEAVY: Drop the flat hands slightly with palms up and hands to the front.

IS: Place right *I* hand at the mouth and move it forward.
LIGHT (weight): Raise the flat hands slightly several times with palms up and hand to the front.
MEASURE: Tap the palm down *Y* hand thumb tips together several times.
ROCK: Hit the back of the closed left hand with the closed right hand. Next, face both *C* hands slightly apart.
SHOULD, NEED, HAVE TO, MUST, NECESSARY: Move

the right bent index down forcefully several times.
THAT: Place the right *Y* hand in the left palm.
WE, US: Touch the right shoulder with the right index finger. Then, circle it forward and back until it touches the left shoulder. The *W* can be used for *we* and *U* for *us*.
WOOD, LUMBER, SAW: Move the edge of the right flat hand back and forth over the back of the left flat hand.

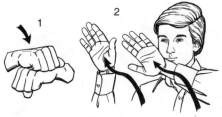  

(mountain) climbing? Protect

   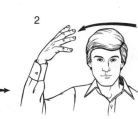

the environment. What a beautiful

tree (rainbow). It

BEAUTIFUL, PRETTY: Place the fingertips of the right *and* hand on the chin. Open the hand as it circles the face from right to left. End with the *and* hand near the chin.

CLIMB: With curved *V* hands facing, make a climbing motion, one hand over the other.

ENVIRONMENT: Move the right *E* hand in a circle around the left vertical index finger.

IT: Touch the right *I* finger in the flat left palm.

MOUNTAIN, HILL: Hit the back of the closed left hand with the closed right hand. Next, make upward wavy movements with both open hands in front of the body.

PROTECT, DEFEND, GUARD: Push both *S* hands forward with palms down and one behind the other.

RAINBOW: Wiggle the fingers of the right open hand in front of the mouth as the hand moves forward. Next, place the right open hand over the head and move it to the right.

THE (definite article): Twist the right *T* hand to the right from a palm-left position.

TREE: Hold the right hand upright with the left hand under the right elbow and wiggle fingers of right hand.

WHAT: Move the tip of the right index finger across the left flat palm.

is   a   bright   sunny   day.

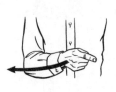  

They   live   near   the

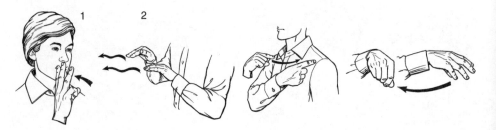

ocean.   We   planted

BRIGHT, CLEAR, LIGHT:
Place the *and* hands in front and move them up and apart to open hands.
DAY: Hold left arm flat, index finger pointing right. Place elbow of bent right arm on left index finger. Move right arm across body in a short arc, index up.
IS: Place the right *I* hand at the mouth and move it forward.
LIVE, ADDRESS: Move *L* hands up chest together.

NEAR, BY, CLOSE TO:
Hold both slightly curved hands to the front and apart, with the right hand near the body. Move right hand near the left hand.
OCEAN: Place the index finger of the right *W* hand on the right side of the mouth several times. Then make forward wavy movements with both curved hands, palms down.
PLANT, SOW: Move the palm-down right curved

hand from left to right as the thumb passes over the inside of the fingers from little to index finger.
SUNNY: Make a left-to-right circle above the head with right index pointing forward.
THEY, THEM, THESE, THOSE: Point forward or to the people or objects with the right index finger and move the hand to the right.
WE, US: *(See page 154.)*

a garden. Keep away

from the bees. My

grass needs cutting.

A: Move the right *A* hand in a small arc to the right.

AWAY: Hold the right curved (or *A*) hand up and move it away from the body to the right. End with the palm facing forward at an upward angle.

BEE: Place the right index finger on right cheek, then brush the right flat-hand fingers forward across cheek.

CUT, SCISSORS: Form *H* fingers with the right hand and open and close them a few times.

FROM: Touch the right *X* index finger on the left vertical index finger and move it back and away.

GARDEN: Move the open hands in a circle in front of body. Hold fingertips of the right *and* hand under one nostril then under the other.

GRASS: Move the right *G* hand to the right while shaking it. Then pass the right *and* hand up and through the left *C* hand while open-ing the fingers.

KEEP: Cross the *V* hands at the wrists, right over left.

MY, MINE, OWN: Place the right flat hand on the chest.

NEED, HAVE TO, MUST, NECESSARY, SHOULD: Move the right bent index finger down forcefully sever-al times.

THE (definite article): Twist the right *T* hand to the right from a palm-left position.

The zoo has <u>monkeys.</u> zebras.

Use one of the following signs.

tigers. giraffes. owls. elephants.

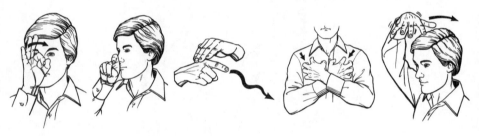

foxes. eagles. snakes. bears. lions.

BEAR: Make clawing movements toward center of the chest with arms crossed.

EAGLE: With palm forward, hold the right *X* hand in front of the nose.

ELEPHANT: Hold the back of the right curved hand at the mouth, palm down, and move it forward a little, then down and up.

FOX, SLY: Place the right *F* hand over the nose and twist toward the left.

GIRAFFE: Put the left *C* hand on the neck. Place the right *C* hand on top of the left, then move right hand forward and upward. Some use the right hand only.

HAS: *(See page 153.)*

LION: Move the right curved open hand over the head as the hand shakes.

MONKEY, APE: Form claw-shaped hands and scratch the sides of the chest.

OWL: Hold the *O* hands up and look through them. Twist the hands back and forth several times.

SNAKE: Pass the right index finger in a weaving movement under left palm.

TIGER: Move the slightly curved hands apart from the center of the face, ending in clawed hands at sides.

ZEBRA: Starting at the center, move the slightly curved open hands across the abdomen, then the chest.

ZOO: Draw the letter *Z* with the right index finger on the left open palm.

CHAPTER 9

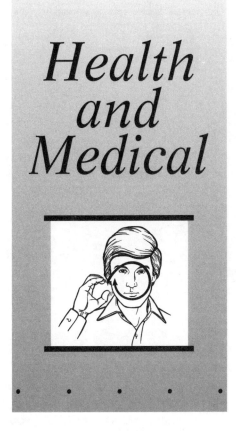

Health and Medical

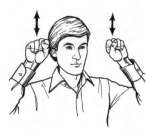   

Exercise daily. Your heart

and blood pressure

 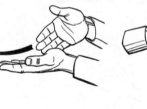  

are OK. Did you

AND: Move right open hand to the right as hand closes with all fingertips touching.
ARE: Move the right *R* hand forward from the lips.
BLOOD, BLEED, HEMOR-RHAGE: Touch the lips with the right index finger. Then, move the wiggling fingers of the right open hand over the back of the left open hand.
DAILY, EVERYDAY: Put right *A* hand on right cheek and slide it forward a few times.
DID, ACTION, DO, DONE:

Move both downturned *C* hands in unison to the left, then to the right.
EXERCISE: Move both *S* hands up and down togeth-er, palms forward.
HEART (physical): Touch the heart area with the right middle finger, keeping other fingers straight.
OK, ALL RIGHT: Slide the right flat-hand edge forward over the entire left flat hand.
PRESSURE: Push the left *G* hand down with the right

flat hand.
YOU: Point to the person you are signing to. Move the right hand from left to right if there is more than one person.
YOUR, YOURS, HIS, HER, THEIR: Push the right flat palm forward toward the per-son being spoken to. If it is not clear from the context, the *male* or *female* sign can be used first. When using *your* in the plural, push the right flat palm forward, then move it to the right.

lose weight (gain weight)? Try eating

l o w - fat foods.

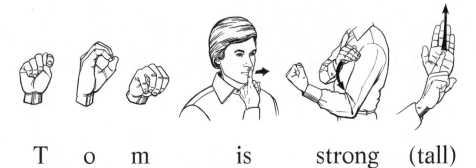

T o m is strong (tall)

EAT, DINE, FOOD, MEAL: Move the fingertips of the right *and* hand to the mouth several times.
FAT, CHUBBY, OBESE: Hold both curved open hands at the cheeks and move them out a few inches to the sides simultaneously.
FOOD: *(See eat above.)*
GAIN WEIGHT, INCREASE: Hold the right *H* fingers palm up and place them on the left palm-down *H* fingers. Repeat several times.

IS: Place the right *I* hand at the mouth and move it forward.
LOSE WEIGHT: Hold the right *H* fingers on top of left *H* fingers and twist the right hand off the left in an arc to the right. Repeat a few times.
STRONG, POWERFUL: Bend the left arm and draw an arc over the left biceps with the right curved hand.
TALL: Slide the right index finger up the flat left hand.

TRY, ATTEMPT, EFFORT: With palms facing, push both *S* hands forward with effort. *Try* and *effort* can be initialized.

(short)   (thin).   I   quit

smoking cigarettes. My breast

exam   was   negative (positive).

BREAST: Touch the left breast, then the right with the fingertips of the right curved hand.

CIGARETTE: Touch the extended left index with the little finger and index finger of the right hand.

EXAMINE, SEARCH: Circle the right *C* hand in front of the face a few times.

I: Place the right *I* hand on the chest with the palm facing left.

MY, MINE, OWN: Place the right flat hand on chest.

NEGATIVE: Hold up the palm-out left flat hand and place the right horizontal index finger against it.

POSITIVE: Make a plus sign with the index fingers.

QUIT, RESIGN: Place right *H* fingers in left *C* hand and quickly pull them out.

SHORT (height), LITTLE, SMALL: Hold bent right hand in front and lower it a little.

SMOKING: Place the right *V* fingers, palm in, in front of the lips.

THIN, LEAN, SKINNY: Move the right index finger and thumb down the cheeks, keeping other fingers closed.

WAS: Move the right *W* hand backward near the right cheek and close it to an *S* hand.

Our   baby   was   born

healthy.   D   e   b   r   a   is

  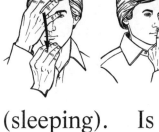 

awake   (sleeping).   Is

AWAKE, WAKE UP: Close the thumbs and index fingers of the *Q* hands at the sides of both eyes. Open the fingers and eyes at the same time.

BABY, INFANT: Pretend to be holding and rocking a baby.

BORN, BIRTH: With palms up, hold the right hand in the left hand and move them forward and up.

HEALTHY, WELL: Place the curved open hands on the chest and move them forward, ending in *S* hands.

IS: Place the right *I* hand at the mouth and move it forward.

OUR: Move the slightly cupped right hand in a semicircle from the right side to the left side of the chest.

SLEEP, NAP: Place the slightly curved right open hand in front of the face and bring it down, ending with the *and* hand at the chin.

WAS: Move the right *W* hand backward near the right cheek and close it to an *S* hand.

your   throat   sore?   How

are   you   feeling?   Are

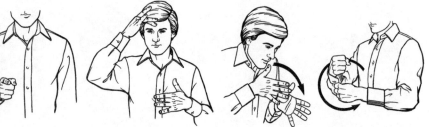

you   sick?   Vomiting? Suffering?

ARE: Move the right *R* hand forward from the lips.

FEELING, SENSATION: Move the right middle finger of the open hand up the chest.

HOW: Place both bent hands together back to back. Turn them forward until the hands are flat, palms up.

SICK, DISEASE, ILL: Touch forehead with the right middle finger and the stomach with the left middle finger.

SORE, SORENESS: Put the tip of the right *A*-hand thumb on the chin and twist it from side to side.

SUFFER, AGONY: Move the right *S* hand slowly in a forward circle around the left *S* hand. The face should express the feeling.

THROAT: Move the right index finger (or *G* fingers) down the throat from under the chin, palm left.

VOMIT, THROW UP: Move the open hands in a forward downward arc from mouth.

YOU: Point to the person you are signing to. Move the right hand from left to right if there is more than one person.

YOUR, YOURS, HIS, HER, THEIR: Push the right flat palm forward toward the person being spoken to. If it is not clear from the context, the *male* or *female* sign can be used first. When using *your* in the plural, push the right flat palm forward, then move it to the right.

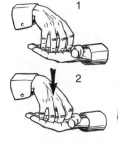

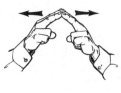

Weak?   I   am   very

ill   (tired).   How   long?

You   don't   look   well.

appear

AM: Move the right *A*-hand thumb forward from the lips.
DON'T, DOESN'T, DO NOT, NOT: Put the right *A*-hand thumb under the chin. Move it quickly forward.
HOW: Place both bent hands together back to back. Turn them forward until the hands are flat, palms up.
I: Place right *I* hand on the chest with palm facing left.
ILL, SICK, DISEASE: Touch the forehead with the right

middle finger and stomach with the left middle finger.
LONG: Move the right index finger up the left arm.
LOOK (appear), FACE: Circle the face with the right index finger.
TIRED, EXHAUSTED: Hold both bent-hands fingertips on the chest. Swivel the hands down, ending with fin- gertips pointing up.
VERY: Place both *V*-hand fingertips together and move them apart.

WEAK: Put the right curved open hand fingers in the left flat palm and bend and unbend the fingers.
WELL, HEALTHY: Place the curved open hands on the chest and move them for- ward ending in *S* hands.
YOU: *(See page 164.)*

Take a pill. Were

 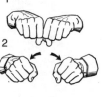 

any bones broken? Don't

touch it. You need

ANY: Hold the right *A* hand with palm in and pointing left. Swing it to a palm-forward position.

BONES: Tap the knuckles of the closed, palm-down, left hand with the right curved index finger.

BROKEN, BREAK, FRACTURE, SNAP: Place the *S* hands to the front and touching. Twist them quickly down and apart like *breaking* a branch.

DON'T: *(See page 167.)*

IT: Touch the right *I* finger in the flat left palm.

NEED, HAVE TO, MUST, NECESSARY, SHOULD: Move the right bent index finger down forcefully several times.

PILL, CAPSULE, TAKE A PILL: Place the right closed thumb and index finger before the mouth and open them as they move toward the mouth.

TAKE: Move the right open hand from right to left, end-ing with a closed hand near the body.

TOUCH: Place the right middle finger on the back of the left hand.

WAS: Move the right *W* hand backward near the right cheek and close it to an *S* hand.

WERE: Hold the right *W* to the front, palm left. Move it backward as it changes to an *R* hand.

YOU: *(See page 167.)*

X rays (oxygen). Don't worry.

Do you have health

(life) insurance? I have

DO, ACTION, DID, DONE: Move both downturned *C* hands in unison to the left, then to the right.
DON'T, DOESN'T, DO NOT, NOT: Put the right *A*-hand thumb under the chin. Move it quickly forward.
HAVE, HAD, HAS, OWN, POSSESS: Move the bent-hands fingertips to the chest.
HEALTH, WELL: Place the curved open hands on the chest and move them for-

ward, ending in *S* hands.
I: Place the right *I* hand on the chest with the palm facing left.
INSURANCE: Shake the right *I* hand back and forth, palm forward.
LIFE: Place the open hands, palms in, on the abdomen and raise the hands to the chest as the fingers wiggle.
OXYGEN: Fingerspell *O* and *2* with right hand. Drop the hand a little for the *2*.

WORRY, ANXIOUS: Move the flat or slightly curved hands in opposite circles in front of the head.
X RAY: Hold up the right *X* hand, palm forward; then make an *and* (or *O*) hand facing self. Thrust the *and* hand at the chest ending with open fingers.
YOU: Point to the person you are signing to. Move the hand from left to right if there is more than one person.

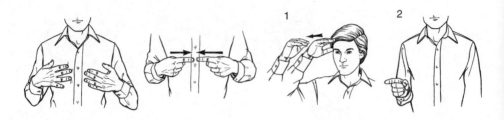

chest   pains.   He

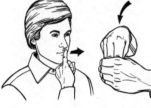 

is   in   the   hospital.   You

need   a   n   operation.   Your

ARE: Move the right *R* hand forward from the lips.
CHEST: Place both open (or one) hands on the chest once or twice.
HE, HIM: Pretend to be gripping a cap with the right hand. Move it forward a little. Then point the index finger forward. If the gender is obvious, omit gripping a cap.
HOSPITAL: Draw a cross on the upper left arm with the right *H* hand.
IN: Place the right *and*-hand

fingertips into the left *C* hand.
IS: Place the right *I* hand at the mouth. Move it forward.
NEED, HAVE TO, MUST, NECESSARY, SHOULD: Move right bent index finger down forcefully several times.
OPERATION, INCISION, SURGERY: Slide the right *A* thumb tip across the chest or stomach area.
PAIN, HURT, ACHE, INJURY: Jab the index fingers at each other a few times in front of the body or

near the pain.
YOU: Point to the person you are signing to. Move the right hand from left to right if there is more than one person.
YOUR, YOURS, HIS, HER, THEIR: Push the right flat palm forward toward the person being spoken to. If it is not clear from the context, the *male* or *female* sign can be used first. When using *your* in the plural, push the right flat palm forward, then move it to the right.

doctor's appointment is J u n e

7 at 3. Are you

allergic to any medicine?

ALLERGIC: Point right index at left *A* thumb and quickly pull both hands apart.

ANY: Hold right *A* hand with palm in and pointing left. Swing it to a palm-forward position.

APPOINTMENT, ENGAGEMENT, RESERVATION: Circle right *A* hand, palm down, over the left *S* hand, palm in. Place the right wrist on the left and move both hands down a little.

ARE: Move the right *R* hand forward from the lips.

AT: Touch right flat-hand fingertips against back of left flat hand, or fingerspell it.

DOCTOR: Hold the right *D* or *M* fingertips on the left pulse.

IS: Place right *I* hand at mouth and move it forward.

MEDICINE, DRUG, PRESCRIPTION: Draw small circles with right middle finger on flat left palm.

SEVEN: Hold up right separated index, middle, and little fingers, palm forward, while touching tips of thumb and ring finger.

THREE: Hold up separated right index, middle finger, and thumb with palm facing forward.

TO: Touch left vertical index fingertip with right index fingertip.

YOU: Point to person you are signing to. Move the right hand from left to right if there is more than one person.

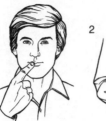

The	bleeding	won't

stop.	Have	you	seen

Doctor	H	i	l	l	before?

BEFORE (time): Hold both slightly curved hands to the front near each other, right behind left. Move the right hand backward.

BLEED, BLOOD, HEMORRHAGE: Touch the lips with the right index finger. Then, move the wiggling fingers of the right open hand over the back of the left open hand.

DOCTOR: Hold the right *D* or *M* fingertips on the left pulse.

HAVE, HAD, HAS, OWN, POSSESS: Move the bent-hands fingertips to the chest.

SEEN: Point the right *V* fingertips toward the eyes. Then move the hand forward.

STOP: Hit the flat left palm with the little-finger edge of the right flat hand.

THE (definite article): Twist the right *T* hand to the right from a palm-left position.

WON'T, REFUSE: Move the right *S* (or *A*) hand quickly back over the right shoulder as the head is turned left.

YOU: Point to the person you are signing to. Move the right hand from left to right if there is more than one person.

   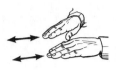

I   can't   breathe   (walk).

My   kids   have   the measles

(mumps).   Get   more   rest.

BREATHE, BREATH: Place both open hands, palms in, and left hand above right, on the chest and move them simultaneously on and off the chest several times.

CANNOT, IMPOSSIBLE, UNABLE: Move the right index finger down, hitting the left index finger as it continues past left finger.

GET: Move the open hands together in front of the body with the right hand on top of the left, forming *S* hands.

HAVE, HAD: Move the bent-hands fingertips to chest.

I: Place right *I* hand on the chest with palm facing left.

KID: Hold the right hand with index and little fingers extended, palm down. Place the index finger under the nose and move the hand up and down slightly.

MEASLES: Place the right curved open-hand fingertips on the right side of the face in several places.

MORE: Bring right *and* hand up to meet left *and* hand, fingertips touching.

MUMPS: Hold the curved open hands at the sides of the neck and move them to the sides a little.

MY, MINE, OWN: Place the right flat hand on the chest.

REST, RELAX: Fold the arms on the chest. *R* hands can be used.

WALK, STEP: Imitate walking by placing both hands palms down and alternately moving each hand forward.

| When | was | your | last |

   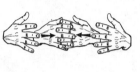

| period? | I | am | pregnant |

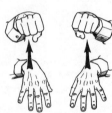 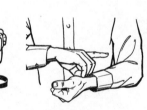 

| (adopted). | The | doctor | will |

ADOPT, ASSUME, TAKE UP: With palms facing down, simultaneously lift up the open hands while closing them into *S* hands.

AM: Move the right *A*-hand thumb forward from the lips.

DID, DO, ACTION, DONE: Move both downturned *C* hands in unison to the left, then to the right.

DOCTOR: Hold the right *D* or *M* fingertips on the left pulse.

I: Place the right *I* hand on chest with palm facing left.

LAST, END, FINAL: Strike the left little finger with the right index finger. Both little fingers can be used.

PERIOD, MENSTRUATION: Hit the right palm side of the *A* hand against the right cheek two times.

PREGNANT: Interlock both open hands on stomach.

WAS: *(See page 166.)*

WHEN: *(See page 173.)*

WILL (verb), SHALL, WOULD: Hold the right flat hand to the right side of the face and move it forward.

YOU: Point to the person you are signing to. Move the right hand from left to right if there is more than one person.

YOUR, YOURS, HIS, HER, THEIR: Push the right flat palm forward toward the person being spoken to. If it is not clear from the context, the *male* or *female* sign can be used first. When using *your* in the plural, push the right flat palm forward, then move it to the right.

examine   you.   Lie down.   The

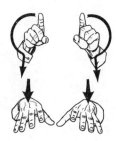
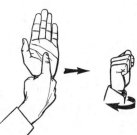

test   revealed   the   sex

o f   the   twins.   Can

CAN, ABILITY, ABLE, COMPETENT, COULD, POSSIBLE: Move both *S* (or *A*) hands down together.
EXAMINE, SEARCH: Circle the right *C* hand in front of the face a few times.
LIE DOWN, RECLINE: Hold the right *V* fingers in the left palm, both palms up.
REVEAL, SHOW: Place the right index finger in the left flat palm and move them forward together.

SEX, INTERCOURSE: Place the *V* hands with palms facing, and move the right hand down on the left several times.
TEST, EXAMINATION, QUIZ: Draw opposite question marks in the air with both index fingers. Then open and move both hands forward.
THE (definite article): Twist the right *T* hand to the right from a palm-left position.

TWINS: Place the right *T* hand at the left side, then the right side of the chin.
WHEN: Move the right index finger around the left upright index finger. Then touch the tip of the right index finger on the tip of the left index finger.
YOU: Point to the person you are signing to. Move the right hand from left to right if there is more than one person.

 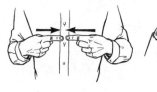 

you   stand?   Does   it

hurt   to   swallow?   Did

you   take   your   cough

COUGH: Hit the chest several times with right curved open-hand fingertips.

DOES, DO, DID, ACTION, DONE: Move both *C* hands, palms down, in unison to the left, then to the right.

HOW: Place both bent hands together back to back. Turn them forward until the hands are flat, palms up.

HURT, ACHE, INJURY, PAIN: Jab the index fingers at each other a few times in front of body or near pain.

IT: Touch the right *I* finger in the flat left palm.

STAND: Stand the right *V* fingers on the flat left palm.

SWALLOW: Move the right index finger down the throat from under the chin, palm left.

TAKE: Move the right open hand from right to left, ending with a closed hand near the body.

TO: Touch the left vertical index fingertip with the right index fingertip.

YOU: Point to the person you are signing to. Move the right hand from left to right if there is more than one person.

YOUR, YOURS, HIS, HER, THEIR: Push the right flat palm forward toward the person being spoken to. If it is not clear from the context, the *male* or *female* sign can be used first. When using *your* in the plural, push the right flat palm forward, then move it to the right.

medicine? How often? Cancel

my appointment. The funeral is

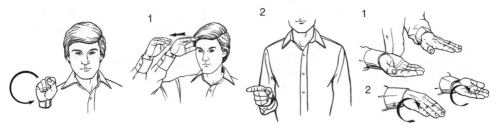

Saturday. He died

APPOINTMENT, ENGAGE-MENT, RESERVATION: Circle right *A* hand, palm down, over left *S* hand, palm in. Place right wrist on the left and move both hands down a little.

CANCEL, CORRECT, CRITICIZE: Draw an *X* on left flat palm with right index finger.

DIE, DEATH, DEAD: Place both flat hands in front with right palm up and left palm down. Twist both hands simultaneously so that right is palm down and left is palm up.

FUNERAL, PARADE: Point both *V* hands up, right behind left, and move them forward together in a couple of short movements.

HE, HIM: Pretend to be gripping a cap with the right hand. Move it forward a little. Then point the right index finger forward. If the gender is obvious, omit gripping a cap.

HOW: *(See page 174.)*

IS: Place the right *I* hand at the mouth and move it forward.

MEDICINE, DRUG, PRE-SCRIPTION: Draw small circles with right middle finger on the flat left palm.

MY: *(See page 171.)*

OFTEN, FREQUENT: Arc the upturned right bent hand into the flat left palm a few times.

SATURDAY: Move the right *S* hand in a small circle.

o f a heart attack.

Is D a w n still

depressed? Her emotions are

A: Move the right *A* hand in a small arc to the right.
ARE: Move the right *R* hand forward from the lips.
DEPRESSED, DISCOUR-AGED: Move both middle fingers down the chest at the same time, while other fingers remain extended.
EMOTION: Move the *E* hands in alternating forward circles as they touch the chest several times.
HEART ATTACK: Touch the heart area with the right

middle finger, keeping other fingers straight. Then strike the left flat palm with the right fist.
HER, SHE: Trace the jaw with the right *A*-hand thumb. Push the flat hand, palm forward, toward the person you are referring to. If the gender is obvious, omit tracing the jaw.
IS: Place the right *I* hand at the mouth and move it forward.
STILL, YET: Move the right

Y hand forward and down a little, palm down.
YOU: Point to the person you are signing to. Move the right hand from left to right if there is more than one person.

better   (worse).   She

has   pneumonia.   Do   you

need   help?   Who   is

BETTER: Place the right flat-hand fingertips on the mouth. Slide it off to an *A* hand at right side of head.

DO, ACTION, DID, DONE: Move both downturned *C* hands in unison to the left, then to the right.

HAS, HAVE, HAD, OWN, POSSESS: Move the bent-hands fingertips to the chest.

HELP, AID, ASSIST: Lift the right *S* hand with the left flat d.

SHE, HER: Trace the jaw with the right *A*-hand thumb. Then point forward. If the gender is obvious, omit tracing the jaw.

IS: Place the right *I* hand at the mouth and move it forward.

NEED, HAVE TO, MUST, NECESSARY, SHOULD: Move the right bent index finger down forcefully several times.

PNEUMONIA: Hold both *P*-hand middle fingers on the chest and move them up and down.

WHO, WHOM: With the right index finger, make a circle in front of the lips.

WORSE, FIGURE, MULTI-PLY: Cross the *V* hands in front of the chest, right behind left.

YOU: Point to the person you are signing to. Move the right hand from left to right if there is more than one person.

   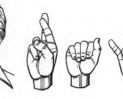

your   doctor   (dentist)?   R   a   y

needs   glasses.   I   feel

dizzy.   Drive   me   to

DENTIST: Place the right *D* thumb on the teeth.

DIZZY: Move the right curved open hand in a few circles in front of the face, palm toward face.

DOCTOR: Hold the right *D* or *M* fingertips on the left pulse.

DRIVE, CAR: Make two *S* hands. Pretend to be steering a car.

FEEL, FEELING, SENSATION: Move the right middle finger of the open hand up the chest.

GLASSES: Hold the right *G-* hand thumb and index finger near the right eye. Slide them back as they close.

I: Place the right *I* hand on the chest with the palm facing left.

ME: Point to or touch the chest with the right index finger.

NEED, HAVE TO, MUST, NECESSARY, SHOULD: Move the right bent index finger down forcefully several times.

TO: Touch the left vertical index fingertip with the right index fingertip.

YOUR, YOURS, HIS, HER, THEIR: Push the right flat palm forward toward the person being spoken to. If it is not clear from the context, the *male* or *female* sign can be used first. When using *your* in the plural, push the right flat palm forward, then move it to the right.

the   hospital.   He

is   restless (quarreling) (drunk).

That   is   poison.   The

DRUNK, INTOXICATE: Swing the right A (or Y)-hand thumb back and down toward the mouth.

HE, HIM: Pretend to be gripping a cap with the right hand. Move it forward a little. Then point the index finger forward. If the gender is obvious, omit gripping a cap.

HOSPITAL: Draw a cross on the upper left arm with the right H hand.

IS: Place the right I hand at mouth and move it forward.

POISON: Move the right P-hand middle finger in small circles in the palm of the left flat hand.

QUARREL: Face both index fingers and move them up and down alternately or in unison.

RESTLESS: Twist the right V hand back and forth in the left palm, palms up.

THAT: Place the right Y hand in the left flat palm.

THE (definite article): Twist the right T hand to the right from a palm-left position.

operation   was   successful.   Don't

cry.   The   nurse   gave

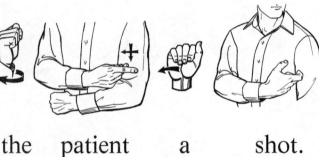

the   patient   a   shot.   Why?

CRY, TEARS, WEEP: Place one or both index fingers under eyes and move them down cheeks several times.
DON'T, DOESN'T, DO NOT, NOT: Put the right A-hand thumb under the chin. Move it quickly forward.
GAVE, GIVE, DISTRIBUTE: Place *and* hands in front, palms down. Move hands forward together, changing to palms-up flat hands.
NURSE: Hold the extended fingertips of right N hand on the pulse area of left wrist.
OPERATION, INCISION, SURGERY: Slide the right A thumb tip across the chest or stomach area.
PATIENT (noun): Draw a cross on the upper left arm with the right P hand.
SHOT, INJECTION: Make the motion of giving a shot with right curved thumb, index, and middle fingers by moving the thumb closer to the curved fingers, which are placed near upper left arm.

SUCCESSFUL, SUCCESS, SUCCEED: Point index fingers at each other. Make simultaneous circles with each hand while moving them upward, ending with both index fingers pointing up, palms forward.
WAS: Move the right W hand backward near right cheek and close it to an S hand.
WHY: Touch the forehead with the right-hand fingertips and move it forward, changing to a Y hand, palm in.

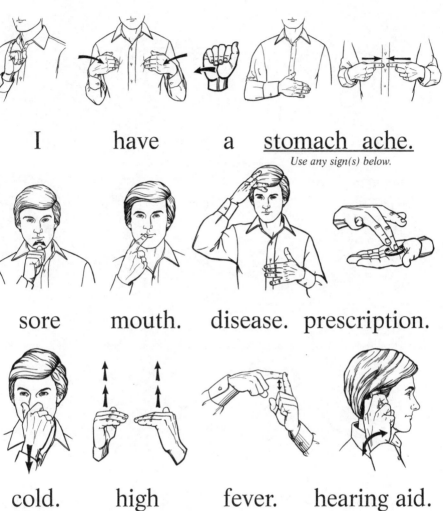

I have a <u>stomach ache.</u>

Use any sign(s) below.

sore mouth. disease. prescription.

cold.
sickness

high fever. hearing aid.

ACHE, HURT, INJURY, PAIN: Jab the index fingers at each other a few times in front of the body or near the pain.
COLD (sickness): Pull the nose down a few times with the right bent index finger and thumb.
DISEASE, SICK, ILL: Touch the forehead with the right middle finger and the stomach with left middle finger.
FEVER, TEMPERATURE, THERMOMETER: Slide the

right index finger up and down the left vertical index finger.
HAVE, HAD, HAS, OWN, POSSESS: Move the bent-hands fingertips to the chest.
HEARING AID: Twist the curved right *V* fingers at the right ear several times.
HIGH, ADVANCED, PRO-MOTION: With the bent hands facing, raise both hands in unison.
I: Place the right *I* hand on

the chest with the palm facing left.
MOUTH: Point to mouth with the right index finger.
PRESCRIPTION, DRUG, MEDICINE: Make small circles with the right middle finger on the flat left palm.
SORE, SORENESS: Put the tip of the right *A*-hand thumb on the chin and twist it from side to side.
STOMACH: Pat the stomach with the right flat hand.

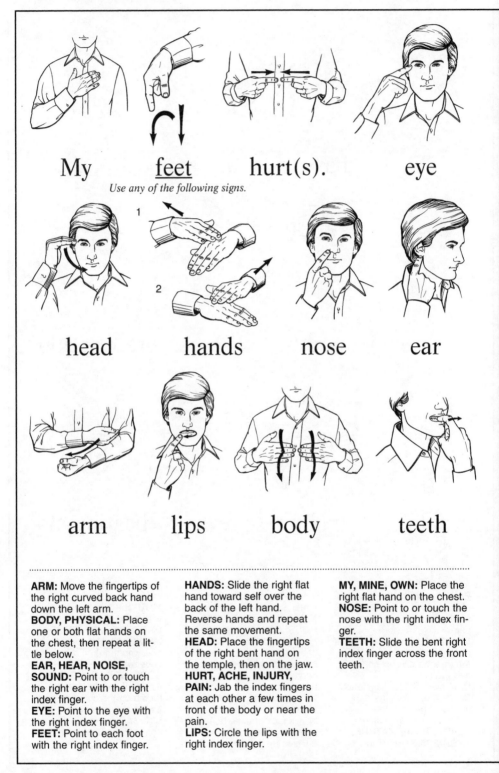

My   <u>feet</u>   hurt(s).   eye

Use any of the following signs.

head   hands   nose   ear

arm   lips   body   teeth

ARM: Move the fingertips of the right curved back hand down the left arm.
BODY, PHYSICAL: Place one or both flat hands on the chest, then repeat a little below.
EAR, HEAR, NOISE, SOUND: Point to or touch the right ear with the right index finger.
EYE: Point to the eye with the right index finger.
FEET: Point to each foot with the right index finger.

HANDS: Slide the right flat hand toward self over the back of the left hand. Reverse hands and repeat the same movement.
HEAD: Place the fingertips of the right bent hand on the temple, then on the jaw.
HURT, ACHE, INJURY, PAIN: Jab the index fingers at each other a few times in front of the body or near the pain.
LIPS: Circle the lips with the right index finger.

MY, MINE, OWN: Place the right flat hand on the chest.
NOSE: Point to or touch the nose with the right index finger.
TEETH: Slide the bent right index finger across the front teeth.

C H A P T E R 10

Emergencies

  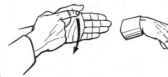

What   happened?   What   did

the   child   eat?   I

am   afraid   (upset)   (nervous).

AFRAID, SCARED: Thrust the *and* hands simultaneously in front of the chest from the sides, one above the other, as they change to open hands.
AM: Move the right *A*-hand thumb forward from the lips.
CHILD, CHILDREN: Hold the right flat hand in front, palm down, and move the hand up and down as if patting a child's head. Repeat the sign to the left (or right) for more then one child.

DID, DO, ACTION, DONE: Move both downturned *C* hands in unison to the left, then to the right.
EAT, DINE, FOOD, MEAL: Move the fingertips of the right *and* hand to the mouth several times.
HAPPEN, EVENT, OCCUR: Hold both index fingers up and to the front with palms facing. Simultaneously pivot both hands to a palm-forward position.
I: Place the right *I* hand on

the chest with the palm facing left.
NERVOUS: Shake the open hands in front of the body, palms down.
UPSET: Hold the right flat hand on the stomach and pivot it to a palm-up position.
WHAT: Move the tip of the right index finger across the left flat palm.

Be   calm   (brave).   It

was   awful.   Hurry,   the

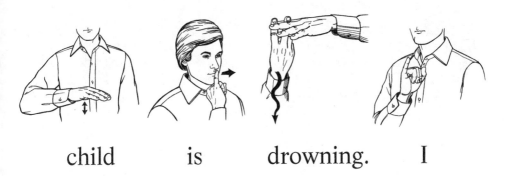

child   is   drowning.   I

AWFUL, FEARFUL, TRAGIC, TERRIBLE: Hold the *O* hands at the temples and fling the fingers forward to open hands, palms facing.
BE: Place the right *B* hand at the mouth and move it forward.
BRAVE: Place both curved open-hand fingertips on the chest, and move them forcefully forward, changing to *S* hands.
CALM, QUIET, SILENT: Place the right index finger on the lips and move both flat hands down and to the sides, palms down.
CHILD, CHILDREN: Hold the right flat hand in front, palm down, and move the hand up and down as if patting a child's head. Repeat the sign to the left (or right) for more then one child.
DROWN: Slip the *V* fingers down through the index and middle fingers of the open left hand in a wavy movement with palm facing body.

HURRY, RUSH: Quickly move right *H* hand up and down in a forward movement.
I: *(See page 184.)*
IS: Place right *I* hand at the mouth and move it forward.
IT: Touch the right *I* finger in the flat left palm.
THE (definite article): Twist the right *T* hand to the right from a palm-left position.
WAS: Move the right *W* hand backward near the right cheek and close it to an *S* hand.

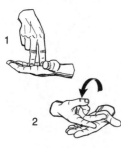

fell (slipped). Who has

authority? Danger. The building is

not safe. I smell

AUTHORITY, ENERGY:
Move the right *A* (or curved) hand in an arc from shoulder to crook of left arm. Use *E* for *energy*.
BUILDING: Alternately place the bent-hand fingers, palms down, on top of each other a few times as they move up a little. Outline the roof and sides of a house with both flat hands, ending with fingers pointing up.
DANGER, PERIL: Push the right *A* thumb up the left *A*

hand several times. Left hand palm faces the body.
FELL, FALL (verb): Place the right *V* fingers upright on the flat left palm. Turn over the *V* hand, laying its back on the flat left palm.
HAS: *(See page 188.)*
I: *(See page 184.)*
IS: *(See page 185.)*
NOT, DON'T: Put the thumb of right *A* hand under chin. Move it quickly forward.
SAFE, FREE, RESCUE, SAVE: Cross the *S* hands

on the chest. Move them out and to the sides as they twist to palm forward. *Free* and *rescue* can be initialized.
SLIP, SLIDE: Move the palm-down right *V* fingers forward across left flat palm.
SMELL, FUMES, ODOR: Move the slightly curved right palm up past the nose a couple of times.
WHO, WHOM: With the right index finger, make a circle in front of the lips.

g   a   s.   Call   9   1   1.

telephone

The   baby   is   choking.

Lock   the   doors.   Hide.

BABY, INFANT: Pretend to be holding and rocking a baby.

CALL, TELEPHONE: Hold the thumb of the right *Y* hand to the ear.

CHOKE, STUCK: Hold the right *V*-hand fingertips at the neck.

DOOR: Place the *B* hands to the front, palms out, and side-by-side. Turn the right hand back and forth.

HIDE: Place the right *A*-hand thumb on the lips and move it forward under the left, palm-down, curved hand.

IS: Place the right *I* hand at mouth and move it forward.

LOCK, KEY, LOCK UP: Twist the right bent index finger to the right on the left flat palm.

NINE-ONE-ONE: Sign *nine* by touching the right thumb with the index finger, other fingers extended, and palm forward. Then, sign *one* by holding up the right index finger pointing slightly forward, and move it to the right in a small arc for the second *one*.

THE (definite article): Twist the right *T* hand to the right from a palm-left position.

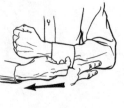

I was robbed. What

was taken? They had

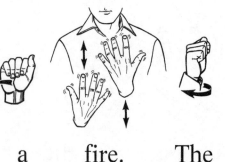

a fire. The electricity is

ELECTRICITY, PHYSICS: With other fingers closed, tap the bent index and middle fingers against each other several times. Index fingers only can be used.

FIRE, BURN, FLAME: Wiggle the slightly curved open-hand fingers up and down in front of the body alternately with palms in.

HAD, HAVE, HAS, OWN, POSSESS: Move the bent hands, placing the fingertips on the chest.

I: Place the right *I* hand on the chest with the palm facing left.

IS: Place the right *I* hand at the mouth and move it forward.

ROB, STEAL: Place the *V* fingers at the left elbow and slide them toward the wrist while curving the *V* fingers.

TAKE: Move the right open hand from right to left, ending with a closed hand near the body.

THEY, THEM, THESE, THOSE: Point forward or to the people or objects with the right index finger and move the hand to the right.

WAS: Move the right *W* hand backward near the right cheek and close it to an *S* hand.

WHAT: Move the tip of the right index finger across the left flat palm.

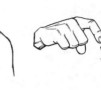

off.   We   need   a

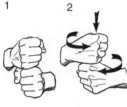

repair   man.   I   lost

my   keys.   Avoid   (guard)

AVOID: Place the *A* hands to the front with the right slightly behind the left, palms facing, and move the right hand backward in a wavy movement.
GUARD, DEFEND: Push both *S* hands forward with palms down and one behind the other.
I: Place the right *I* hand on chest with palm facing left.
KEY, LOCK, LOCK UP: Twist right bent index finger to right on left flat palm.

LOST, LOSE: Touch the fingertips of both *and* hands. Then drop them as the hands open.
MAN: Place the right open-hand thumb on the forehead and chest.
MY, MINE, OWN: Place the right flat hand on the chest.
NEED, HAVE TO, MUST, NECESSARY, SHOULD: Move the right bent index finger down forcefully several times.
OFF: Move the flat right

hand up a few inches off the back of the flat left hand, palms down.
REPAIR, MAKE, FIX: Hit the left *S* hand with the right *S* hand. Twist the hands in. Then repeat.
WE, US: Touch the right shoulder with the right index finger. Then, circle it forward and back until it touches the left shoulder. The *W* can be used for *we* and *U* for *us*.

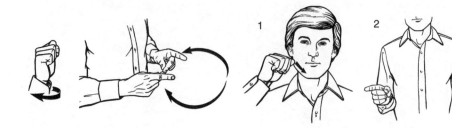

the   area.   She

disappeared. Tornado   warning.   They

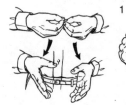  

lost   everything   in   the

AREA, LOCATION, PLACE: Touch the *P*-hand fingers, palms facing, to the front and move them back in opposite semicircles, touching fingers again near the body. *Location* and *place* may be initialized.
DISAPPEAR: Hold the right vertical index finger between the thumb and index finger of the left flat hand and pull it down.
EACH, EVERY: Rub right *A*-hand knuckles down the left

A-hand thumb a few times.
EVERYTHING: Rub the right *A*-hand knuckles down the left *A*-hand thumb a few times. Drop the slightly curved flat hand in front of body and move it to right.
IN: Place right *and*-hand fingertips into the left *C* hand.
LOST, LOSE: Touch the fingertips of both *and* hands. Drop them as hands open.
HER, SHE: Trace the jaw with the right *A*-hand thumb. Then point forward. If the

gender is obvious, omit tracing the jaw.
THEY: (See page 188.)
TORNADO: Point the right index finger down and the left index finger up and rotate them in small circles around each other. *T* hands can be used. Also, hands can move up and to the right as they rotate.
WARNING, CAUTION: Hit the right flat hand against the back of the left flat hand a couple of times.

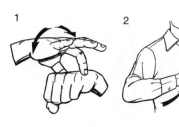 

earthquake   (flood).

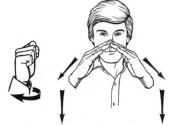  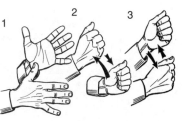

The   house   was   destroyed.

 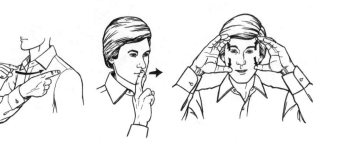

We   are   shocked (disappointed).

ARE: Move the right *R* hand forward from the lips.
DESTROY, DAMAGE: Place the open hands in front, palms facing, the left hand higher than the right. Reverse the hands, changing to *A* hands. Reverse them again, keeping the *A*-hand shapes.
DISAPPOINT: Touch the chin with the tip of the right index finger.
EARTHQUAKE: Hold the left closed hand between the right index finger and thumb and rock the right hand from left to right. Move with force both *S* hands alternately forward and backward in front of the body.
FLOOD: Sign *water* first by touching the right side of the mouth with the index finger of the right *W* hand several times. Next, place the open hands in front, palms down, and wiggle the fingers as both hands are raised together.
HOUSE: Outline the shape of a house with the flat hands.
SHOCK: Suddenly open the *C* hands to a wider *C* in front of the eyes.
WAS: Move the right *W* hand backward near right cheek and close it to an *S* hand.
WE, US: Touch the right shoulder with the right index finger. Then, circle it forward and back until it touches the left shoulder. The *W* can be used for *we* and *U* for *us*.

 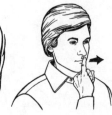  

| There | is | a | car |

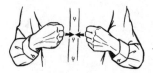

| accident. | But, | no | people |

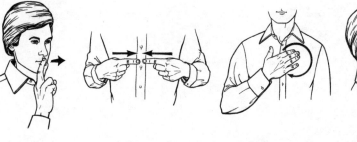

| are | hurt. | Please | don't |

ACCIDENT, COLLISION, CRASH, WRECK: Hit both *S* hands head on.

ARE: Move the right *R* hand forward from the lips.

BUT, HOWEVER: With palms out, cross the index fingers, then pull them apart.

CAR, DRIVE: Make two *S* hands. Pretend to be steering a car.

DON'T, NOT: Put the thumb of the right *A* hand under the chin. Move it quickly forward.

HURT, ACHE, INJURY, PAIN: Jab the index fingers at each other a few times in front of body or near pain.

NO, NONE: Place the *O* hands to the front with fingers touching. Move them apart in opposite directions.

PEOPLE: Move the *P* hands in alternating, inward circles in front of the body.

PLEASE, ENJOY, LIKE, PLEASURE: Put the right hand over the heart and move it in a small circle.

THERE: Point with the right index finger to an imaginary object.

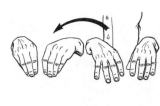

move   (fear).   Trust

me.   He   revived.

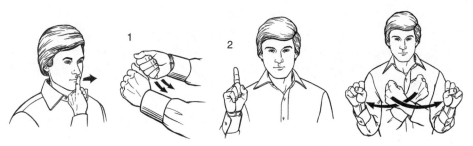

Is   everyone   safe?

EVERYONE, EVERYBODY: Rub the right *A*-hand knuckles down the left *A*-hand thumb a few times. Then sign the number one.

FEAR, TERROR: Place both open hands in front, right slightly behind left, with palms forward; move them back in a shaking motion.

HE, HIM: Pretend to be gripping a cap with the right hand. Move it forward a little. Then point the right index finger forward. If the gender is obvious, omit gripping a cap.

ME: Point to or touch the chest with the right index finger.

MOVE, PUT: Hold the open curved hands to the left front, palms down. Move them together up and down to the right while closing them to *and* hands.

REVIVE: Move both *R* hands up the chest.

SAFE, FREE, RESCUE, SAVE: Cross the *S* hands on the chest. Move them out and to the sides as they twist to palms forward. *Free* and *rescue* can be initialized.

TRUST, CONFIDENCE: Hold slightly curved open hands to front and pull them in to body, changing to *S* hands, right under left near the left shoulder.

Call
telephone

the **police**.
Use any sign(s) below.

hospital.

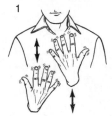

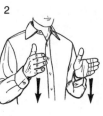

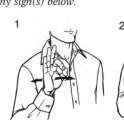

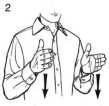

firefighters.

minister.

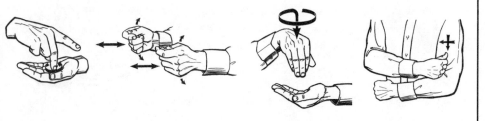

poison   control   center. ambulance.

AMBULANCE: Draw a cross on the upper left arm with the right *A* thumb.

CALL, TELEPHONE: Hold the thumb of the right *Y* hand to the ear.

CENTER, CENTRAL, MIDDLE: Circle the right curved hand, palm down, above the left. Then place the right into the left palm.

CONTROL, OPERATE, RULE: Move both modified *A* hands (thumbs in crooks of index fingers) alternately back and forth, palms facing. Wrists can move up and down a little.

FIREFIGHTER: Wiggle the slightly curved open-hand fingers up and down in front of the body alternately with palms in. Add the *person-ending* sign.

HOSPITAL: Draw a cross on the upper left arm with the right *H* hand.

MINISTER, PASTOR: Move the right *F* hand forward and backward in front of the right shoulder a few times, palm forward. Add the *person-ending* sign.

POISON: Move the right *P*-hand middle finger in small circles in the palm of the left flat hand.

POLICE, COP, SHERIFF: Hold the right *C* hand at the left shoulder.

THE (definite article): Twist the right *T* hand to the right from a palm-left position.

CHAPTER 11

Education

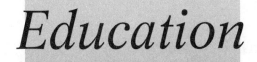

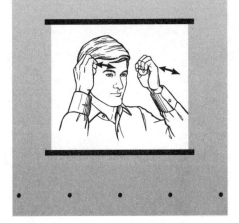

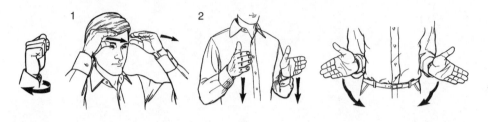

The   teacher   encouraged

(influenced)   me.   He

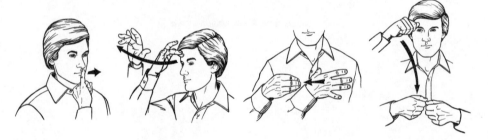

is   smart   and   remembers

AND: Move the right open hand to the right as hand closes to all fingertips touching.
ENCOURAGE: Point both flat (or open) hands slightly to the sides and move them forward in short movements as if pushing.
HE, HIM: Pretend to be gripping a cap with the right hand. Move it forward a little. Then point the right index finger forward. If the gender is obvious, omit grip-ping a cap.
INFLUENCE: Place the right *and* hand on the back of the flat left hand. Then move the *and* hand forward as it changes to an open hand and circles the flat left hand below.
IS: Place the right *I* hand at mouth and move it forward.
ME: Point to or touch the chest with the right index finger.
REMEMBER: Place the right *A*-hand thumb on the forehead, then on the left *A*-hand thumb.
SMART, BRILLIANT, CLEVER, INTELLIGENT: Touch the forehead with the middle finger of the right open hand. Then turn the hand forward and up. Some use the index finger.
TEACHER: Place both open *and* hands in front of the forehead facing each other. Move them forward, ending with *and* hands. Then make the *person-ending* sign.

everything.   Teach   me

(them).   Complete   the   lesson.

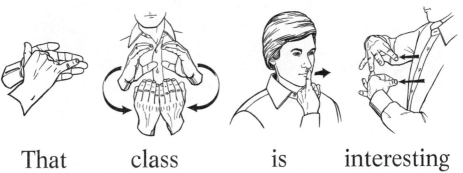

That   class   is   interesting

CLASS, GROUP, AUDI-ENCE: Place the *C* hands palms facing and move them in a forward circle until hands touch. *Audience* and *group* can be initialized.
COMPLETE, DONE, END, FINISH: Slide the flat right hand off the edge of the left flat hand and down.
EVERYTHING: Rub right *A*-hand knuckles down left *A*-hand thumb a few times. Then, drop the slightly curved flat hand in front of

body and move it to right.
INTERESTING, INTEREST: Hold both hands with open index fingers and thumbs on the chest, other fingers extended, right above left. Move them forward, closing the thumb and index fingers.
IS: Place right *I* hand at the mouth and move it forward.
LESSON: Rest the edge of the right flat hand across the fingers of the left flat hand and move it in a small arc to the base of left palm.

ME: Point to or touch chest with the right index finger.
TEACH, EDUCATE, INSTRUCT: Place both open *and* hands in front of the forehead facing each other. Move them forward, ending with *and* hands.
THAT: Place the right *Y* hand in the left flat palm.
THEM, THEY, THESE, THOSE: Point forward or to the people or objects with the right index finger and move the hand to the right.

(boring).   What   do   you

think?   Give   me   your

attention.   The   rules   seem

ATTENTION, CONCENTRATION, FOCUS, PAY ATTENTION: Place both flat hands, palms facing, at the sides of the face. Move them forward together.
BORING, MONOTONOUS: Place the tip of the right index finger on the side of the nose and twist it forward.
DO: *(See page 202.)*
GIVE, DISTRIBUTE: Place *and* hands in front, palms down, and move the hands forward together, changing to palms-up flat hands.
ME: *(See page 197.)*
RULES, REGULATIONS: Move the right *R* hand in an arc down the left flat hand from fingertips to the base.
SEEM, APPEAR: Place the right curved hand before the face, palm left; twist it until palm faces self as you look at palm.
THINK, CONSIDER: Circle right index finger at forehead.
WHAT: Move the tip of the right index finger across the left flat palm.
YOU: Point to person you are signing to. Move the right hand from left to right if there is more than one person.
YOUR, YOURS, HIS, HER, THEIR: Push the right flat palm forward toward the person being spoken to. If it is not clear from the context, the *male* or *female* sign can be used first. When using *your* in the plural, push the right flat palm forward, then move it to the right.

 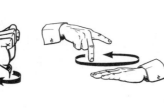 

unfair.   The   principal   used

 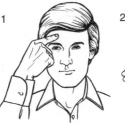 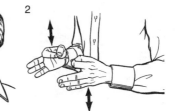

good   judgment.   The

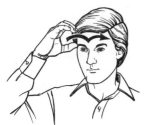

computer   made   the   search

COMPUTER: With the right *C* hand, make a double arc from right to left in front of the forehead.

GOOD, WELL: Touch the lips with the right flat hand. Bring the right hand down into the left hand, palms up.

JUDGE, COURT, JUDGEMENT, JUSTICE, TRIAL: Place the right index finger on the forehead. Move the two *F* hands, palms facing, alternately up and down.

MADE, MAKE: Hit the left *S* hand with the right *S* hand. Twist hands in. Then repeat.

PRINCIPAL: With palms down, circle the right *P* hand over the left flat hand.

SEARCH, EXAMINE: Circle the right *C* hand in front of the face a few times.

THE (definite article): Twist the right *T* hand to the right from a palm-left position.

UNFAIR: Strike the fingertips of the left *F* hand with the fingertips of right *F* hand.

USED, USE: Make a circle with the right *U* hand, palm forward.

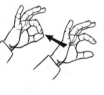

easy. Choose another subject

to write about. I

am curious. Can I

ABOUT, CONCERNING: Point the left *and* hand to the right and circle it with the right index finger.
AM: Move the right *A*-hand thumb forward from the lips.
ANOTHER, OTHER: Hold right *A*-hand thumb palm left, and twist it to right, palm up.
CAN, ABILITY, ABLE, COMPETENT, COULD, POSSIBLE: Move both *S* (or *A*) hands down together.
CHOOSE, PICK, SELECT: Hold the right open thumb

and index forward, other fingers extended. Move the hand back as the thumb and index touch, as if picking out an item.
CURIOUS: Grasp a little skin in front of neck. Move it slightly from side to side.
EASY, SIMPLE: Place the left curved hand in front with palm up. Move the right curved hand up several times, brushing the little-finger side against the fingertips of the left hand.

I: Place the right *I* hand on chest with palm facing left.
MY, MINE, OWN: Place the right flat hand on the chest.
SUBJECT, QUOTE, TITLE: Place the curved *V* hands in front, palms forward, and twist them to palms facing each other.
TO: Touch the left vertical index fingertip with the right index fingertip.
WRITE: Pretend to write on left flat palm with right index finger and thumb.

help   you   with   your

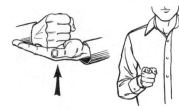
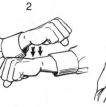

homework?   I   know   the

correct   answer.   Fingerspell   it.

....

ANSWER, REPLY, RESPOND: Place the right index finger in front of the lips and the left vertical index finger in front of the right. Move both hands in an arc until both index fingers point forward.

CORRECT, RIGHT: Face the index fingers forward with the right above the left and bring the right hand down on the left hand.

FINGERSPELL: Move the fingers up and down as the right open hand moves from left to right with palm down.

HELP, AID, ASSIST: Lift the right *S* hand with the left flat hand.

HOMEWORK: Touch the right *and-*hand fingertips on the mouth then on the right cheek. Next, tap the right *S-*hand wrist on the left *S-*hand wrist several times, palms down.

I: *(See page 200.)*

IT: Touch the right *I* finger in the flat left palm.

KNOW, INTELLIGENCE, KNOWLEDGE, RECOGNIZE: Touch the fingertips of the right hand on the forehead several times.

WITH: Place both *A* hands together, palms facing.

YOU: Point to the person you are signing to. Move the right hand from left to right if there is more than one person.

YOUR: *(See page 198.)*

 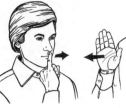 

| What | is | your | science |

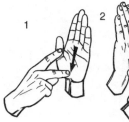 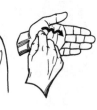

| project? | Did | you | write |

| your | paper | (poetry)? | Stop |

DID, ACTION, DO, DONE: Move both *C* hands, palms down, in unison to the left, then to the right.

IS: Place the right *I* hand at the mouth and move it forward.

PAPER: Hit the heel of the right flat hand against the heel of the left flat hand two times from right to left.

POETRY, POEM: Swing the right *P* hand back and forth in front of the left flat hand.

PROJECT: Slide the right *P*-hand middle finger down the left flat palm. Twist the left hand and slide the right *J*-hand little finger down the back of it.

SCIENCE, BIOLOGY, CHEMISTRY, EXPERIMENT: Move the extended *A*-hand thumbs alternately in and down a few times in front of the chest. Initialize *biology*, *chemistry*, and *experiment*.

STOP: Hit the flat left palm with the little-finger edge of the right flat hand.

WHAT: Move the tip of the right index finger across the left flat palm.

WRITE: Pretend to be writing on the left flat palm with the closed right index finger and thumb.

YOU: Point to the person you are signing to. Move the right hand from left to right if there is more than one person.

YOUR: *(See page 198.)*

procrastinating. Did you pass

(fail) the test? That is

 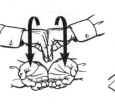

difficult (worthless). How is

....

DID, ACTION, DO, DONE: Move both downturned *C* hands in unison to the left, then to the right.
DIFFICULT, HARD: Hit the bent *V*-hand knuckles against each other as the hands move up and down.
FAIL: Place right *V* hand in left flat hand, both palms up, and slide it across, off, and down a little.
HOW: Place bent hands together back to back. Turn them forward until the hands

are flat, palms up.
IS: *(See page 202.)*
PASS: Hold the *A* hands with right slightly behind left and move the left hand ahead of the right.
PROCRASTINATE, DELAY: Place *F* hands in front and move them forward in small arcs with palms facing.
TEST, EXAMINATION, QUIZ: Draw opposite question marks in the air with both index fingers. Then open and move both hands

forward.
THAT: Place the right *Y* hand in the left palm.
WORTHLESS, USELESS: Swing the *F* hands together from the sides. Then move the hands to the sides as they open.
YOU: Point to the person you are signing to. Move the right hand from left to right if there is more than one person.
YOUR: *(See page 198.)*

 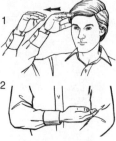 

my   son   (daughter)   doing

 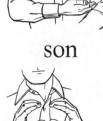 

in   class?   The   library

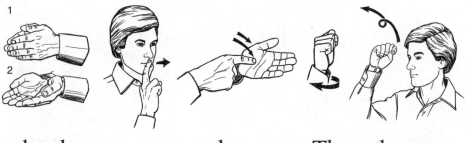

books   are   due.   The   theory

ARE: Move the right *R* hand forward from the lips.
BOOK: Close both flat hands palm to palm, then open them.
CLASS, GROUP, AUDIENCE: Place the *C* hands palms facing and move them in a forward circle until the hands touch. *Audience* and *group* can be initialized.
DAUGHTER: Slide the right *A*-hand thumb along the right side of the jaw to the chin. Then place the right flat hand, palm up, in the fold of the bent left arm.
DUE, DEBT, OWE: Touch the left flat palm with the right index finger a few times.
DO, ACTION, DID, DONE: Move both *C* hands, palms down, in unison to the left, then to the right.
IN: Place right *and*-hand fingertips into the left *C* hand.
LIBRARY: Move the right *L* hand to the right in a small circle, palm forward.

MY, MINE, OWN: Place the right flat hand on the chest.
SON: Pretend to grip a cap and move the right hand forward a little. Place the right flat hand, palm up, in the crook of the bent left arm.
THEORY, IMAGINATION, FANTASY: Move the right *T* hand forward and up in a few circles in front of the forehead, palm in. Use *I* hand for *imagination*; *F* hand for *fantasy*.

   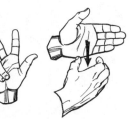

| is | stupid. | Read | three | chapters. |

   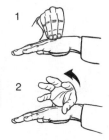

| Give | me | your | advice. |

| When | is | the | final |

ADVICE, ADVISE, COUNSEL: Hold the right *and*-hand fingertips on the back of the left flat hand. Thrust right hand forward as it changes to an open hand.
CHAPTER: Slide the right *C*-hand thumb and fingers down horizontal left palm.
FINAL, END, LAST: Strike the left little finger with the right index finger. Both little fingers can be used.
GIVE, DISTRIBUTE: Place the *and* hands in front,

palms down. Move hands forward together, changing to palms-up flat hands.
IS: *(See page 206.)*
ME: Point to or touch the chest with right index finger.
READ: Point the right *V* fingers at the left flat hand and move the *V* hand down.
STUPID: Hit the right *A* (or *S*) hand, palm in, against the forehead several times.
THREE: Hold up right index, middle finger, and thumb with palm facing forward.

WHEN: Move the right index finger around the left upright index finger. Then touch the tip of the right index finger on the tip of the left index finger.
YOUR, YOURS, HIS, HER, THEIR: Push the right flat palm forward toward the person being spoken to. If it is not clear from the context, the *male* or *female* sign can be used first. When using *your* in the plural, push the right flat palm forward, then move it to the right.

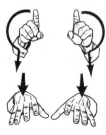 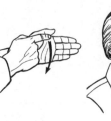  

exam?   What   is   on   the

  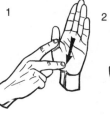 

test?   Check   the   program

schedule.   Is   there   a

A: Move the right *A* hand in a small arc to the right.

CHECK, INSPECT, INVESTIGATE: Point to the right eye, then move the right index finger over the left flat palm and past the fingers.

EXAMINATION, QUIZ, TEST: Draw opposite question marks in the air with both index fingers. Then open and move both hands forward.

IS: Place the right *I* hand at mouth and move it forward.

ON: Place the right flat hand on top of the left flat hand, palms down.

PROGRAM: Slide the right *P*-hand middle finger down the palm and back of the left flat hand. Twist the left hand so observer can see second movement.

SCHEDULE: Slide the right open hand, palms facing, down across the left hand. Next, slide the back of the right hand over the left hand from palm to fingertips.

TEST: *(See examination at left.)*

THE (definite article): Twist the right *T* hand to the right from a palm-left position.

THERE: Point with the right index finger to an imaginary object.

WHAT: Move the tip of the right index finger across the left flat palm.

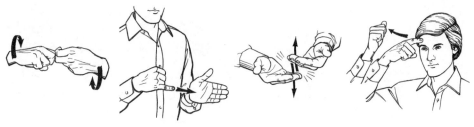

problem?　　It　doesn't matter　because

I　　　studied.　　What　　did

you　　learn?　　Memorize　the

BECAUSE: Touch forehead with the right index finger, palm in, and move it slightly up and right to an *A* hand.
DID, ACTION, DO, DONE: Move both downturned *C* hands in unison to the left, then to the right.
DOESN'T MATTER, ALTHOUGH, ANYHOW: Move the fingertips of both slightly curved hands up and down over each other several times with palms up.
I: Place the right *I* hand on the chest with the palm facing left.
IT: Touch the right *I* finger in the flat left palm.
LEARN: Hold the open right-hand fingertips on the left flat hand. Next, move the right hand up, changing to an *and* hand ending with the *and*-hand fingertips on the forehead.
MEMORIZE: Touch the forehead with right index finger, palm in, and move it forward, changing to an *S* hand.

PROBLEM: Twist the bent *U* (or *V*)-hand knuckles back and forth in opposite directions as they touch each other.
STUDY: Wiggle the fingers of the right open hand as the hand moves back and forth in front of the left flat hand.
WHAT: *(See page 206.)*
YOU: Point to person you are signing to. Move the right hand from left to right if there is more than one person.

vocabulary.   I   misunderstood

(don't know).   What   are   your

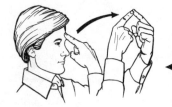

goals?   Your   education   is

ARE: Move the right *R* hand forward from the lips.
DON'T KNOW, DIDN'T RECOGNIZE: Touch the fingertips of the right flat hand on the forehead and flip the hand as it moves forward a little, palm out.
EDUCATION: Hold both *E* hands near the forehead, palms facing, and move them ahead and back several times.
GOAL, AMBITION: Touch the forehead with the right

index finger, then touch the left index finger, which is held a little higher than the head with palm in.
I: Place the right *I* hand on the chest with the palm facing left.
IS: Place the right *I* hand at the mouth and move it forward.
MISUNDERSTOOD: Touch the forehead with the right *V*-hand middle finger, palm in. Then twist the hand and touch the index finger to the

forehead, palm forward.
THIS: Place the right index finger in the left flat palm for something specific.
VOCABULARY: Hold the palm-forward right *V* fingers against the left index finger.
WHAT: Move the tip of the right index finger across the left flat palm.
YOUR: *(See page 205.)*

important. Explain this word.

Get the dictionary. We

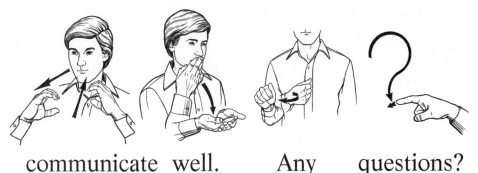

communicate well. Any questions?

ANY: Hold the right *A* hand with palm in and pointing left. Swing it to a palm-forward position.

COMMUNICATE: Move both *C* hands alternately back and forth from the mouth, palms facing.

DICTIONARY: Shake the right *D* hand, palm forward.

EXPLAIN, DEFINE, DESCRIBE: Hold the *F* hands to the front, palms facing, and close together. Move them alternately back and forth. *Define* and *describe* can be signed with *D* hands.

GET: Move the open hands together in front of the body with the right hand on top of the left, forming *S* hands.

IMPORTANT, PRECIOUS, VALUABLE: Move the *F* hands, from palms up to palms down, to the center of the body until fingers touch.

QUESTION, QUESTION MARK: Draw a question mark in the air with the right index finger. Include the period.

THIS: *(See page 208.)*

WE: *(See page 191.)*

WELL, GOOD: Touch the lips with the right flat hand. Bring the right hand down into the left hand, palms up.

WORD: Place the right *Q* fingertips on the vertical left index finger, which faces palm left.

We   need   more   information.

I'm   finished   (busy).

 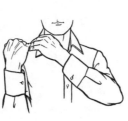  

Whose responsibility   is   it?

AM: Move the right *A*-hand thumb forward from the lips.
BUSY: Place the right *B*-hand wrist, palm forward, on the wrist of the palm-down left closed hand. Move the right *B* hand back and forth as it taps the left wrist.
FINISH, ALREADY, COMPLETE: Place the open hands in front, palms facing the body and fingers pointing up. Twist them to the sides several times.
I: Place the right *I* hand on the chest, palm left.
INFORMATION, INFORM: Hold both *and*-hand fingers on the forehead. Move them forward and down to palms-up open hands.
IS: Place the right *I* hand at the mouth and move it forward.
IT: Touch the right *I* finger in the flat left palm.
MORE: Bring the right *and* hand up to meet the left *and* hand, fingertips touching.
NEED, HAVE TO, MUST, NECESSARY, SHOULD: Move the right bent index finger down forcefully several times.
RESPONSIBILITY, BURDEN, OBLIGATION: Hold both curved-hand fingers on right shoulder. *R* hands can be used for *responsibility*.
WE: *(See page 191.)*
WHOSE, WHO, WHOM: With the right index finger, make a circle in front of the lips.

  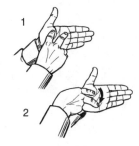

What do you mean?

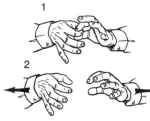 

Class dismissed. Read the

story. Practice. Don't be

BE: Place right *B* hand at mouth and move it forward.
CLASS, GROUP, AUDIENCE: Place the *C* hands palms facing and move them in a forward circle until the hands touch. *Audience* and *group* can be initialized.
DISMISS, LAID OFF: Quickly brush the right flat-hand fingers over and off the lower part of the left flat hand.
DO, ACTION, DID, DONE: Move both downturned *C* hands in unison to the left then to the right.
DO NOT, DOESN'T, NOT: Put the right *A*-hand thumb under the chin. Move it quickly forward.
MEAN (verb), INTEND, PURPOSE: Place right *V* fingers in left palm. Remove and twist them to the right and place them again in the left palm.
PRACTICE: Move the right *A*-hand knuckles back and forth over the left index finger.

READ: Point the right *V* fingers at the left flat hand and move the *V* hand down.
STORY: Join the *F*-hand fingers like two links in a chain and separate them to the sides a few times.
WHAT: Move the tip of the right index finger across the left flat palm.
YOU: *(See page 207.)*

lazy.   Register   tomorrow.   Can

you   speechread?   The   speech

was   good.   What   school

CAN, ABILITY, ABLE, COMPETENT, COULD, POSSIBLE: Move both *S* (or *A*) hands down together.
GOOD, WELL: Touch the lips with the right flat hand. Bring the right hand down into the left hand, palms up.
LAZY: Place the right *L* hand, palm in, on the left shoulder once or twice.
REGISTER, SIGNATURE: Move the upturned right *H* fingers into the flat left palm.
SCHOOL: Clap twice.

SPEECH, LECTURE: Move the slightly curved right hand forward and backward at the right a few times.
SPEECHREAD, LIPREAD, ORAL: Circle the curved *V* fingers in front of the mouth.
TOMORROW: Place the right *A* thumb on the right cheek or chin area and move it forward in an arc.
WAS: Move the right *W* hand backward near the right cheek and close it to an *S* hand.

WHAT: Move the tip of the right index finger across the left flat palm.
YOU: Point to the person you are signing to. Move the right hand from left to right if there is more than one person.

(college)   did   you   go

to?   My   major   is

psychology   (math)   (history).   Is

COLLEGE: Clap the hands once, then circle the right flat hand over the left flat hand.
DID, ACTION, DO, DONE: Move both downturned C hands in unison to the left, then to the right.
GO: Circle the index fingers around each other as they move forward.
HISTORY: Swing the right H hand up and down a little.
IS: Place the right I hand at mouth and move it forward.

MAJOR, SPECIALTY: Move the right flat-hand edge along the top edge of the left flat hand.
MATHEMATICS, ALGE-BRA, GEOMETRY: Hold the M hands with palms facing and cross the hands, right behind left. Initialize *algebra* and *geometry*.
MY, MINE, OWN: Place the right flat hand on the chest..
PSYCHOLOGY: Hold the left flat hand with palm somewhat forward and hit

the area between the thumb and index finger with the lower edge of the right flat hand once or twice.
TO: Touch the left vertical index fingertip with the right index fingertip.
YOU: Point to the person you are signing to. Move the right hand from left to right if there is more than one person.

it   true   or   false?

The   curriculum   improved.   Try

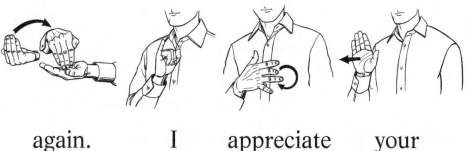

again.   I   appreciate   your

AGAIN, REPEAT: Turn the bent right hand up and into the flat left palm.
APPRECIATE: Circle right middle finger over the heart, other fingers extended.
CURRICULUM: Slide the right *C* hand down the left vertical flat hand, changing to an *M* hand.
FALSE, FAKE: Move the vertical right index finger across lips from right to left.
I: Place the right *I* hand on the chest with the palm

facing left.
IMPROVE: Move the right flat hand up the left arm in small arcs starting at the wrist.
IT: Touch the right *I* finger in the flat left palm.
OR, EITHER: Touch the left *L*-hand thumb and index finger several times with the right index finger.
TRUE, REAL: Move the right index finger forward in an arc from the lips, palm left.

TRY, ATTEMPT, EFFORT: With palms facing, push both *S* hands forward with effort. *Try* and *effort* can be initialized.
YOUR, YOURS, HIS, HER, THEIR: Push the right flat palm forward toward the person being spoken to. If it is not clear from the context, the *male* or *female* sign can be used first. When using *your* in the plural, push the right flat palm forward, then move it to the right.

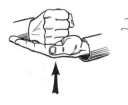   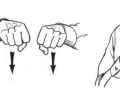  

help.   Can   I   still

get   into   your   course?

I   need   to   study.

CAN, ABILITY, ABLE, COMPETENT, COULD, POSSIBLE: Move both *S* (or *A*) hands down together.
COURSE: Move the right *C* hand from the fingers to the palm of the left flat hand.
GET: Move the open hands together in front of the body with the right hand on top of the left, forming *S* hands.
HELP, AID, ASSIST: Lift the right *S* hand with the left flat hand.
I: Place the right *I* hand on

the chest with the palm facing left.
INTO, ENTER: Thrust right *and* hand down through the left *C* hand and out.
NEED, HAVE TO, MUST, NECESSARY, SHOULD: Move the right bent index finger down forcefully several times.
STILL, YET: Move the right *Y* hand forward and down a little, palm down.
STUDY: Wiggle the fingers of the right open hand as

the hand moves back and forth in front of left flat hand.
TO: Touch the left vertical index fingertip with the right index fingertip.
YOUR, YOURS, HIS, HER, THEIR: Push the right flat palm forward toward the person being spoken to. If it is not clear from the context, the *male* or *female* sign can be used first. When using *your* in the plural, push the right flat palm forward, then move it to the right.

I   am   a <u>graduate.</u> freshman.

Use any of the following signs.

sophomore. junior.   senior.   volunteer.

student.   [a   n]   assistant.

A: Move the right *A* hand in a small arc to the right.
AM: Move the right *A*-hand thumb forward from the lips.
ASSISTANT: Place the right *L*-hand thumb under the left closed hand.
FRESHMAN: Touch the left open-hand ring finger with the right index finger.
GRADUATE: Circle the right *G* hand above the left flat hand and place it into the left flat palm.
I: Place the right *I* hand on the chest with the palm facing left.
JUNIOR: Place the right index finger on the left open-hand index finger.
SENIOR: With the right index finger, touch the left open-hand thumb .
SOPHOMORE: Place the right index finger on the middle finger of the left open hand.
STUDENT: Place the right open-hand fingers on the flat left palm. Move the right hand, to the forehead as the fingers close to an *and* hand, ending with fingertips on the forehead. Add the *person-ending* sign.
VOLUNTEER, APPLY, CANDIDATE: Grab the shirt near the right shoulder between the index finger and thumb of the right hand and pull it once or a few times. The lapel of a shirt or collar of a dress can be used.

CHAPTER 12

Religion

I   enjoyed   the   sermon.

He   is   a

missionary.   I   believe

BELIEVE: Touch the forehead with the right index finger; then place both hands together, right on left, in front of the chest.

ENJOY, PLEASE, LIKE, PLEASURE: Put the right hand over the heart and move it in a small circle.

HE, HIM: Pretend to be gripping a cap with the right hand. Move it forward a little. Then point the right index finger forward. If the gender is obvious, omit gripping a cap.

I: Place the right *I* hand on the chest with the palm facing left.

IS: Place the right *I* hand at the mouth and move it forward.

MISSIONARY: Move the right *M* hand in a circle over the heart. Add the *person-ending* sign.

SERMON, PREACH: Move the right *F* hand back and forth near the right shoulder a few times.

THE (definite article): Twist

the right *T* hand to the right from a palm-left position.

YOU: Point to the person you are signing to. Move the right hand from left to right if there is more than one person.

 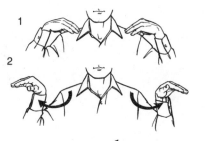 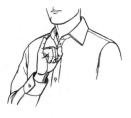

in   angels.   I

admire   your   convictions.   Were

you   baptized?   God   bless

ADMIRE, LIKE: Hold the thumb and index finger of right open hand on chest. Move hand forward, closing thumb and index finger.
ANGEL, WINGS: Touch the shoulders, then turn both hands outward and flap the hands a few times. One hand can be used.
BAPTIZE, BAPTISM, BAPTIST: Place the *A* hands in front, palms facing. Then move and twist the hands so that the thumbs point right

and slightly down.
BLESS: Place both *A*-hand thumbs at the lips. Move the hands forward and downward, changing to flat hands, palms down.
CONVICTIONS, CONSCIENCE: Shake right index up and down near the heart.
GOD: Point the right *G* hand upward (or flat hand). Move it down to the chest ending in a *B* hand.
I: *(See page 218.)*
IN: Place the right *and*-hand

fingertips into left *C* hand.
WERE: Hold right *W* to the front, palm left. Move it back as it changes to an *R* hand.
YOU: *(See page 220.)*
YOUR, YOURS, HIS, HER, THEIR: Push the right flat palm forward toward the person being spoken to. If it is not clear from the context, the *male* or *female* sign can be used first. When using *your* in the plural, push the right flat palm forward, then move it to the right.

  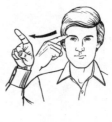 

you.   Interpret   for   me.

Be   faithful   (humble).   The

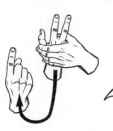     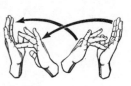

trinity   is   God,   Jesus,

BE: Place the right *B* hand at the mouth and move it forward.

FAITHFUL: Strike the left *F* hand a few times with the right *F* hand while moving both hands forward.

FOR: Place the right index finger at the right temple. Twist it forward as the hand moves forward.

GOD: Point the right *G* hand (or flat hand) upward. Move it down to the chest, ending in a *B* hand.

HUMBLE: Place the right *B* hand at the lips and move it under the flat left hand, which is held to the front with palm down. The head can be bowed at same time.

INTERPRET: Place the left *F* hand, palm forward, before the right *F* hand, palms facing. Reverse the hands so right palm is forward.

IS: Place the right *I* hand at the mouth and move it forward.

JESUS: Place both hands to the front with palms facing. Touch the right middle finger to the left palm; then touch the left middle finger to the right palm.

ME: Point to or touch the chest with right index finger.

TRINITY: Cup the right *3* hand in the left *C* hand, then pull the right hand down and up to a *1* hand.

YOU: Point to the person you are signing to. Move the right hand from left to right if there is more than one person.

   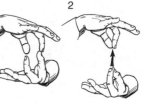

| and | the | Holy | Spirit. |

   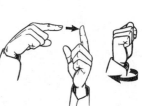

| Tithing | is | important | to | the |

| church. | Don't | lie | (cheat). |

AND: *(See page 223.)*
CHEAT, DECEIVE, FRAUD: Face left *Y* hand forward with the index finger extended and palm down. Make the same hand shape with right hand and slide it back and forth over the top of the left hand several times.
CHURCH, CHAPEL: Touch the right *C*-hand thumb on the back of the left *S* hand.
DON'T, DOESN'T, DO NOT, NOT: Put the right *A*-hand thumb under the chin. Move it quickly forward.
HOLY, DIVINE, RIGHT-EOUS: Form a right *H* hand, then pass the right flat hand across the left flat hand. *Note:* Initialize each word.
IMPORTANT, PRECIOUS, VALUABLE: Move the *F* hands, from palms up to palms down to the center of the body until fingers touch.
LIE: Push the right index finger across the lips from right to left.
SPIRIT, GHOST: Place the right hand over the left hand, palms facing. Close the index fingers and thumbs of both hands (making *F* hands) as the right hand moves up.
TITHE: Sign 1/10. Point the right index finger up. Then form an *A* hand a little lower and shake it back and forth a little.
TO: *(See page 229.)*
YOUR: *(See page 225.)*

 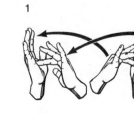 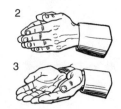

Read   the   Bible.

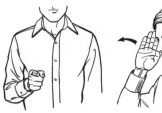 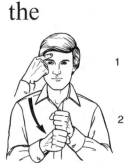  

Have   faith.   Repent   and

you   will   be   forgiven.

AND: Move the right open hand to the right as the hand closes to all fingertips touching.

BE: Place the right *B* hand at the mouth and move it forward.

BIBLE: Place both hands to the front with palms facing. Touch the left palm with the right middle finger; then touch the right palm with the left middle finger. Close both flat hands palm to palm, then open them.

FAITH: Put the right index finger on the forehead. Move both hands to the front, right under left, closing them to *S* hands.

FORGIVE, EXCUSE, PARDON: Move the right fingertips over the lower part of left flat hand a few times.

HAVE, HAD, HAS, OWN, POSSESS: Move the bent-hands fingertips to the chest.

READ: Point the right *V* fingers at the left flat hand and move the *V* hand down.

REPENT: Cross the *R* hands at the wrists with palms facing, right over left. Then switch positions with left hand over right.

WILL (verb), SHALL, WOULD: Hold the right flat hand to the right side of the face and move it forward.

YOU: Point to the person you are signing to. Move the right hand from left to right if there is more than one person.

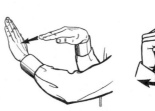

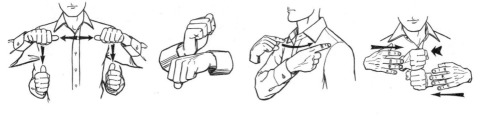

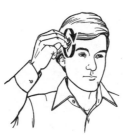

| Praise | God. | Kneel | and |

| pray | (meditate) | at | the |

| altar | (temple). | We | received |

ALTAR: Hold the *A* hands in front with thumbs touching. Move them apart sideways, then down with palms facing.
AND: Move right open hand to the right as the hand closes to all fingertips touching.
AT: Touch the right flat-hand fingertips against the back of the left flat hand, or finger-spell it.
GOD: Point the right *G* hand (or flat hand) upward. Move it down to the chest, ending in a *B* hand.

KNEEL, PROTESTANT: Place right bent *V* fingers in left flat palm as if kneeling.
MEDITATE: Place the right *M* hand near the right temple and make forward circles.
PRAISE, CLAP: Clap the hands a few times or as much as wanted.
PRAY: Place both flat hands together; then simultaneously bow and move the hands toward self.
RECEIVE: Hold the open

hands in front and bring them together while forming *S* hands, placing the right on top of left. Move both hands toward the body.
TEMPLE (building): Hold the base of the right *T* hand on the back of palm-down left closed hand.
WE, US: Touch the right shoulder with the right index finger. Then, circle it forward and back until it touches the left shoulder. The *W* can be used for *we* and *U* for *us.*

  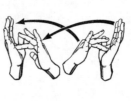 

communion. Jesus was

crucified (sacrificed) on

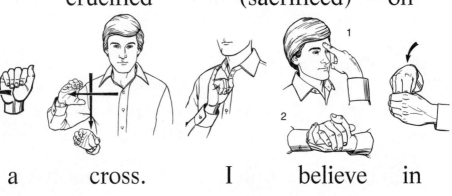

a cross. I believe in

BELIEVE: Touch the forehead with the right index finger; then place both hands together, right on left, in front of the chest.

COMMUNION: Place the flat left hand in front of the body. Move the little finger of the right hand down over the back of the left hand a few times. Move the right *W* hand over the right cheek in a forward circular movement.

CROSS (noun): Draw a cross with the right *C* hand, first down, then across.

CRUCIFY, CRUCIFIXION: Touch the left open-hand palm with the right index finger; then strike the left palm with the bottom of the right closed hand. Hold both flat hands up, palms out.

I: *(See page 226.)*

IN: Place the right *and*-hand fingertips into left *C* hand.

JESUS: Place both hands to the front with palms facing. Touch the right middle

finger to the left palm; then touch the left middle finger to the right palm.

ON: Place the right flat hand on top of the left flat hand, palms down.

SACRIFICE: Move the *S* hands up and forward to flat hands, palms up.

WAS: Move the right *W* hand backward near the right cheek and close it to an *S* hand.

the resurrection.   It   was

a   miracle.   Confess

your   sins.   Are   you

A: Move the right *A* hand in a small arc to the right.
ARE: Move the right *R* hand forward from the lips.
CONFESS, ADMIT: Place the fingers of both hands on chest, pointing down. Move them forward to palms up.
IT: Touch the right *I* finger in the flat left palm.
MIRACLE, MARVEL: Push both open hands forward and upward several times. Hit the right *S*-hand wrist on the top of the left *S*-hand

wrist several times.
RESURRECTION: Move the right *V* hand, from a palm-up to palm-down position with the fingertips standing in the left flat palm.
SIN, EVIL: Hold both index fingers pointing at each other and make simultaneous circles.
WAS: Move the right *W* hand backward near the right cheek and close it to an *S* hand.
YOU: Point to the person

you are signing to. Move the right hand from left to right if there is more than one person.
YOUR, YOURS, HIS, HER, THEIR: Push the right flat palm forward toward the person being spoken to. If it is not clear from the context, the *male* or *female* sign can be used first. When using *your* in the plural, push the right flat palm forward, then move it to the right.

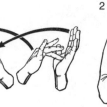  

a Christian? Where

do you worship? Hallelujah.

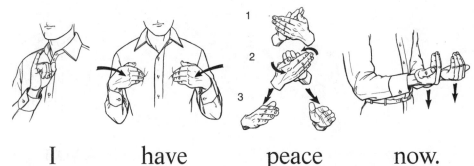

I have peace now.

CHRISTIAN: Place both hands to the front with palms facing. Touch the left palm with the right middle finger; then touch the right palm with left middle finger. Add the *person-ending* sign.
DO, ACTION, DID, DONE: Move both *C* hands, palms down, in unison to the left, then to the right.
HALLELUJAH: Clap the hands and circle the right modified *A* hand a few times near the head.

HAVE, HAD, HAS, OWN, POSSESS: Move the bent-hands fingertips to the chest.
I: Place the right *I* hand on the chest, palm left.
NOW, CURRENT, IMMEDI-ATE: Quickly drop both bent (or *Y*) hands in front of the body at the waist, palms up.
PEACE: Put the right flat hand on left flat hand, then the left on the right with palms down. Move both flat hands down and to sides.

WHERE: Shake the right index finger back and forth.
WORSHIP: Cover the right closed hand with the left hand and move the hands close to the body. Head can bow.
YOU: Point to the person you are signing to. Move the right hand from left to right if there is more than one person.

Passover   starts   tomorrow.   Adam

  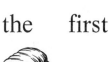

and   Eve   were   the   first

man   and   woman.   The

ADAM: Touch the right *A*-hand thumb to the temple.
AND: Move the right open hand to the right as the hand closes to all fingertips touching.
EVE: Place the right *E* hand at the right side of the chin, palm out.
FIRST: Touch the extended left thumb with the right index finger.
MAN: Place the right open-hand thumb on the forehead and chest.

PASSOVER: Hit the left elbow several times with the right *P* fingers.
START, BEGIN: Twist the right *one*-hand index finger in the *V* shape of the flat left hand.
THE (definite article): Twist the right *T* hand to the right from a palm-left position.
TOMORROW: Place the right *A* thumb on the right cheek or chin area and move it forward in an arc.
WAS: Move the right *W*

hand backward near the right cheek and close it to an *S* hand.
WERE: Hold the right *W*, palm left, to the front. Move it backward as it changes to an *R* hand.
WOMAN: Place the right open-hand thumb on the chin, then on the chest.

  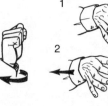 

gospels   tell   the   story

o   f   Christ.   Are   you

(fasting)   in   the   ministry? The

ARE: Move the right *R* hand forward from the lips.
CHRIST, LORD, KING: Place the right *C* hand at the left shoulder and move it to the right waist. Initialize *Lord* and *King*.
FASTING: Slide the right *F*-hand thumb and index finger from left to right over the mouth.
GOSPEL: Move the right *G* hand across the left flat hand a few times from fingertips to wrist.

IN: Place the right *and*-hand fingertips into the left *C* hand.
MINISTRY: Hit the left wrist with the wrist of the right *M* hand a couple of times, palms down.
STORY: Join the *F*-hand fingers like two links in a chain and separate them to the sides a few times.
TELL, SAY, SPEAK, SPEECH: Move the right index finger in a forward circle from the mouth.

THE (definite article): Twist the right *T* hand to the right from a palm-left position.
YOU: Point to the person you are signing to. Move the right hand from left to right if there is more than one person.

rabbi   (nun)   said   to

obey   the   commandments. The

priest   spoke   about   heaven

ABOUT, CONCERNING: Point the left *and* hand to the right and circle it with the right index finger.

COMMANDMENTS: Place the right *C* hand on the vertical left flat fingers and move the *C* hand down to the palm.

HEAVEN: Place both flat hands to the front with palms in. Move them in a circle toward the body. Pass the right hand under the left as the hands move up and cross in front of forehead.

NUN: Outline a semicircle with the right *N* hand by going up the left side, across the forehead, then down the right side of the face.

OBEY: Place *A* hands on forehead. Then move them down to the front with the flat hands turned palms up.

PRIEST, CHAPLAIN: Move the right *Q* fingers along the right side of neck starting at the front.

RABBI: Slide the *R* fingers down the chest together, palms in.

SAID, SAY, SPEAK, SPEECH, TELL: Move the right index finger in a forward circle from the mouth.

SPOKE: *(See said above.)*

TO: Touch the left vertical index fingertip with the right index fingertip.

THE (definite article): Twist the right *T* hand to the right from a palm-left position.

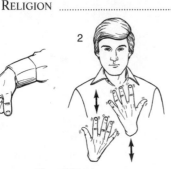

(hell). The devil

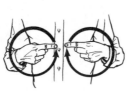

is evil. Don't be

selfish (vain) (jealous). I

BE: Place the right *B* hand at the mouth and move it forward.
DEVIL, DEMON, SATAN: Place the right *3*-hand thumb at the temple with palm forward and bend and unbend the index and middle fingers several times.
DON'T, DOESN'T, DO NOT, NOT: Put the right *A*-hand thumb under the chin. Move it quickly forward.
EVIL, SIN: Hold both index fingers pointing at each other and make simultaneous circles.
HELL: Point the right index finger down. Alternately move the slightly curved open hands up and down in front of the body while wiggling the fingers, palms in.
I: Place the right *I* hand on the chest with the palm facing left.
IS: Place the right *I* hand at the mouth and move it forward.
JEALOUS: Twist the little finger of the right *J* hand at the right corner of the mouth.
SELFISH, GREEDY: Place the *V* fingers forward and pull them back, bending the fingers simultaneously.
THE (definite article): Twist the right *T* hand to the right from a palm-left position.
VAIN (characteristic), VANITY: Hold both *V* hands in front, palms in, and bend and unbend the fingers together several times.

 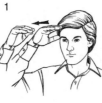 

pity   him.   Revenge

    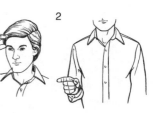

(envy)   is   wrong.   He

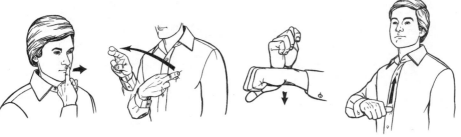

is   religious (traditional) (proud).

ENVY: Move the right index fingertip from side to side between the teeth several times.
HE: *(See him below.)*
HIM, HE: Pretend to be gripping a cap with the right hand. Move it forward a little. Then point the right index finger forward. If the gender is obvious, omit gripping a cap (the sign for *male*).
IS: Place the right *I* hand at the mouth. Move it forward.

PITY, COMPASSION, MERCY: Slide the right middle finger up the chest, other fingers extended. Make a couple of forward circles with the right hand in the same shape, palm down.
PROUD: Slide the extended right *A*-hand thumb up the chest, palm down.
RELIGIOUS, RELIGION: Touch the right *R* fingers at the heart and twist palm forward and up in an arc.

REVENGE: Hold the thumbs and index fingertips of both hands together, other fingers closed. With palms facing, tap the index fingers and thumbs together a few times in front of the body.
TRADITIONAL, TRADITION: Place the right *T*-hand wrist on the left *S*-hand wrist and move both down a little.
WRONG, ERROR, MISTAKE: Hold the right *Y* hand on the chin, palm in.

  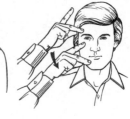 

Respect   your   parents.   Don't

steal   (gossip).   She

 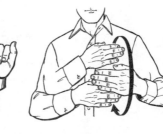

is   a   kind   (mean)

DON'T: *(See page 233.)*
GOSSIP: Open and close the *Q* fingers and thumbs near the mouth a few times.
IS: Place the right *I* hand at the mouth. Move it forward.
KIND (emotion): Hold the left flat hand to the front. Place the right flat hand on the heart. Next, circle the right hand around the left hand, over and under.
MEAN (adjective), CRUEL: Move the right bent *V* knuckles down, hitting the

left bent *V* knuckles.
PARENTS: Touch the right temple with the right *P*-hand middle finger, then the right side of the chin.
RESPECT, HONOR: Move the right *R* hand down toward the face in an arc. The head can be bowed at the same time. Use the *H* hand for *honor*.
SHE, HER: Trace the jaw with the right *A*-hand thumb. Then point forward. If the gender is obvious, omit trac-

ing the jaw (the *female* sign).
STEAL, ROB: Place the right *V* fingers at left elbow and slide them toward wrist while curving the *V* fingers.
YOUR, YOURS, HIS, HER, THEIR: Push the right flat palm forward toward the person being spoken to. If it is not clear from the context, the *male* or *female* sign can be used first. When using *your* in the plural, push the right flat palm forward, then move it to the right.

person.	Are	you	lonely?

  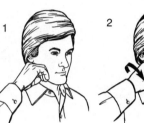

Don't	be	ashamed.

  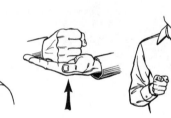

God	will	help	you.

ARE: Move the right *R* hand forward from the lips.
ASHAMED, SHAME: With palm facing down, hold the back of the right bent hand on the right cheek. Twist the hand forward so palm faces back.
BE: Place the right *B* hand at the mouth and move it forward.
DON'T, DOESN'T, DO NOT, NOT: Put the right *A*-hand thumb under the chin. Move it quickly forward.

GOD: Point the right *G* hand (or flat hand) upward. Move it down to the chest, ending in a *B* hand.
HELP, AID, ASSIST: Lift the right *S* hand with the left flat hand.
LONELY, LONESOME: Move the right index finger down across the lips once or twice. Palm faces left.
PERSON: Move the *P* hands down together.
WILL (verb), SHALL, WOULD: Hold the right flat

hand to the right side of the face and move it forward.
YOU: Point to the person you are signing to. Move the right hand from left to right if there is more than one person.

I am <u>**Baptist.**</u> Catholic.

Use any of the following signs.

Presbyterian. Jewish. Lutheran. Episcopal.

Assemblies of God. Methodist. Protestant.

AM: Move the right *A*-hand thumb forward from the lips.
ASSEMBLIES OF GOD: Place the right *A*-hand thumb on the forehead; then point the *G* hand (or flat hand) upward. Move the right hand to the chest, forming a *B* hand.
BAPTIST, BAPTISM: Place the *A* hands in front, palms facing. Then move and twist the hands so that the thumbs point right and slightly down.

CATHOLIC: Draw a cross in front of the forehead with the right *U* fingers.
EPISCOPAL: Place the left arm and closed hand to the front. Touch the bottom of the left wrist with the right index finger. Then, move the right index in an arc to the left elbow.
I: Place the right *I* hand on the chest, palm left.
JEWISH: Touch the chin with the right open hand and move it down to an *and* hand.

LUTHERAN: Place the right *L* thumb in the vertical left palm.
METHODIST, AMBITIOUS, ANXIOUS, EAGER, ENTHU-SIASTIC: Eagerly rub the flat hands together.
PRESBYTERIAN: Place the middle finger of the right *P* hand in the palm of the left flat hand.
PROTESTANT, KNEEL: Place the right bent *V* fingers in the left flat palm as if kneeling.

Business
and
Government

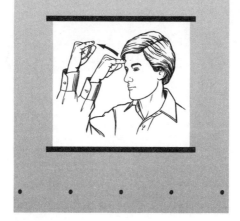

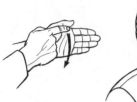 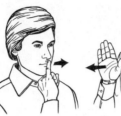  

What   is   your   profession?

He   is   a n

expert.   You   did   a n

DID, ACTION, DO, DONE: Move both *C* hands, palms down, in unison to the left, then to the right.
EXPERT, SKILLFUL: Point the left flat hand up, palm right, and hold it with the right hand. Move the right hand forward off the left.
HE, HIM: Pretend to be gripping a cap with the right hand. Move it forward a little. Then point the right index finger forward. If the gender is obvious, omit gripping a cap.

IS: Place the right *I* hand at the mouth and move it forward.
PROFESSION, PROFESSIONAL: Slide the right *P*-hand fingers along the edge of the index finger of the left flat hand.
WHAT: Move the tip of the right index finger across the left flat palm.
YOU: Point to the person you are signing to. Move the right hand from left to right if there is more than one person.

YOUR, YOURS, HIS, HER, THEIR: Push the right flat palm forward toward the person being spoken to. If it is not clear from the context, the *male* or *female* sign can be used first. When using *your* in the plural, push the right flat palm forward, then move it to the right.

 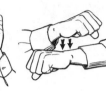  

excellent   job.   We   earned

a   profit.   The   boss   wants

you   to   work   late

....

BOSS, CAPTAIN, CHAIRMAN, OFFICER: Hold the right curved open hand on the right shoulder.
EARN, COLLECT, SALARY, WAGES: Move the right curved hand across the left flat hand. The right hand can end in a closed position.
EXCELLENT, WONDERFUL: Push both flat open hands forward and up several times, palms out.
JOB, WORK: Tap the right

S-hand wrist on the left S-hand wrist several times, palms down.
LATE, NOT YET: Move the right flat hand back and forth a few times near the right side.
PROFIT, BENEFIT, GAIN: Move the right F-hand thumb and index finger into an imaginary pocket on the left side of the chest.
TO: Touch the left vertical index fingertip with the right index fingertip.

WANT, DESIRE: Hold both curved open hands with palms up. Move both hands toward the body a few times.
WE, US: Touch the right shoulder with the right index finger. Then, circle it forward and back until it touches the left shoulder. The *W* can be used for *we* and *U* for *us*.
WORK, JOB: Tap the right S-hand wrist on the left S-hand wrist several times, palms down.
YOU: *(See page 236.)*

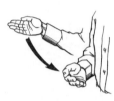   

if　　　possible.　　Were　　　you

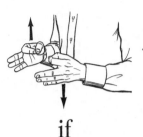  

hired?　Where?　　It　　　is　　　a

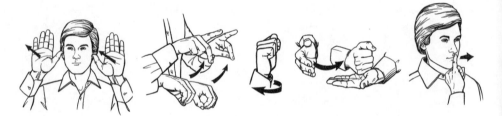

fantastic　opportunity.　The　　salary　　is

FANTASTIC, EXCELLENT, WONDERFUL: Push both flat open hands forward and up several times, palms out.

HIRE, EMPLOY, INVITE: Move the right flat hand (or *H* hand) toward the body, from the right side, palm up.

IF: Move the *F* hands, palms facing, alternately up and down.

IS: Place the right *I* hand at the mouth and move it forward.

IT: Touch the right *I* finger in the flat left palm.

OPPORTUNITY: Place the *O* hands to front, palms down, and move them up to *P* hands.

POSSIBLE, ABILITY, ABLE, CAN, COMPETENT, COULD: Move both *S* (or *A*) hands down together.

SALARY, WAGES: Move the right curved hand across the left flat hand. The right hand can end in a closed position.

WERE: Hold the right *W* to the right front, palm left. Move it backward as it changes to an *R* hand.

WHERE: Shake the right index finger back and forth, palm forward.

YOU: Point to the person you are signing to. Move the right hand from left to right if there is more than one person.

  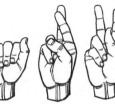 

good.　　M　a　r　k　　was

fired　　(laid off)　(rehabilitated). The

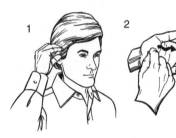 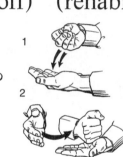 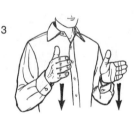

secretary　　　　(treasurer)

FIRED, DISCHARGED, EXPELLED: Swing the right flat hand, palm up, sharply across the top of the left *S* hand.

GOOD, WELL: Touch the lips with the right flat hand. Bring the right hand down into the left hand, palms up.

HE, HIM: Pretend to be gripping a cap with the right hand. Move it forward a little. Then point the right index finger forward. If the gender is obvious, omit gripping a cap.

LAID OFF, DISMISS: Quickly brush the right flat-hand fingers over and off the lower part of the left flat hand.

REHABILITATE: Hold the left flat hand to the front, palm up. Place the right *R* hand on top of the left hand and lift both hands together.

SECRETARY: Take an imaginary pencil from over the right ear and pretend to be writing on the flat left palm with the right index fin-

ger and thumb, other fingers closed.

TREASURER: Sign *money* by tapping the back of the right *and* hand in the left palm a few times. Next, sign *collect* by moving the right curved hand across the left flat hand, ending in a closed hand. Then add the *person-ending* sign.

WAS: Move the right *W* hand backward near the right cheek and close it to an *S* hand.

  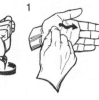 

quit.   Call   the   reporter

 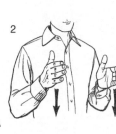  

(photographer).   Don't   disturb

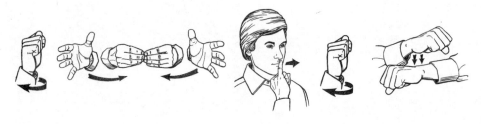

the   meeting.   Is   the   job

CALL, SUMMON: Place the right slightly curved hand on the back of the left flat hand. Move the right hand up toward the body, ending with an *A* hand.

DISTURB, INTERFERE: Hit the flat right hand between the thumb and index finger of the left hand several times.

DON'T, DOESN'T, DO NOT, NOT: Put the right *A*-hand thumb under the chin. Move it quickly forward.

IS: Place the right *I* hand at the mouth and move it forward.

JOB, WORK: Tap the right *S*-hand wrist on the left *S*-hand wrist several times, palms down.

MEETING, ASSEMBLE, GATHER: Hold the open hands apart and to the sides. Move them together closing them to *and* hands with fingertips touching.

PHOTOGRAPHER: Move the right *C* hand from the right cheek and place it against the vertical flat hand. Add the *person-ending* sign.

QUIT, RESIGN: Place the right *H* fingers in the left *C* hand and quickly pull them out.

REPORTER, WRITER: Pretend to be writing on the left palm with the thumb and index finger of the right hand (other fingers closed). Sign the *person ending* by moving the flat hands down.

done?

We

are

not

enemies.

The

strike

has   ended.   Send   it

ARE: Move the right *R* hand forward from the lips.
DONE, COMPLETE, END, FINISH: Slide the flat right hand off the edge of the left flat hand and down.
END: *(See done above.)*
NOT, DON'T: Put the thumb of the right *A* hand under the chin. Move it quickly forward.
ENEMY, OPPONENT, RIVAL: Point both index finger at each other, then quickly pull them apart. Add

the *person-ending* sign.
HAS, HAD, HAVE, OWN, POSSESS: Move the bent-hands fingertips to the chest.
IT: Touch the right *I* finger in the flat left palm.
SEND: Place the right bent-hand fingertips on the back of the left bent hand and flip the fingers forward and up, ending with a right flat hand.
STRIKE, REBEL: Place the right *S* hand near the right side of the face, palm in,

and twist the hand to palm forward.
WE, US: Touch the right shoulder with the right index finger. Then, circle it forward and back until it touches the left shoulder. The *W* hand can be used for *we* and *U* hand for *us*.

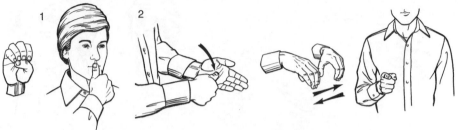

E - mail. Do you

like my idea? F a x

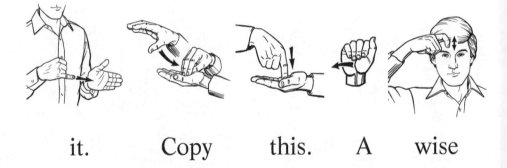

it. Copy this. A wise

A: Move the right *A* hand in a small arc to the right.

COPY, DUPLICATE, IMITATE: Place the open right hand into the left flat palm, ending with the *and* hand.

DO, DID, ACTION, DONE: Move both *C* hands, palms down, in unison to the left, then to the right.

IDEA: Touch the right *I*-hand finger on the forehead and move it upward, palm in.

IT: Touch the right *I* finger in the flat left palm.

LIKE, ADMIRE: Hold the thumb and index finger of the right open hand on the chest. Move the hand forward, closing the thumb and index finger.

MAIL, LETTER: Put the thumb of the right *A* hand on the lips; then place it on the left flat palm.

MY, MINE, OWN: Place the right flat hand on the chest.

THIS: Place the right index finger in the left flat palm for something specific.

WISE, WISDOM: Move the right *X* hand up and down in front of the forehead.

YOU: Point to the person you are signing to. Move the right hand from left to right if there is more than one person.

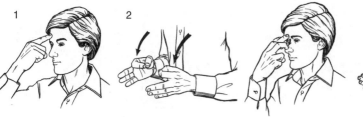

decision.   I doubt it.   Ask

a   lawyer.   Reject the

offer.   The   machine   is

A: Move the right *A* hand in a small arc to the right.
ASK, REQUEST: Place the flat hands together and move them toward you.
DECISION, DECIDE: Place the right index finger to the forehead. With palms facing, move both *F* hands down.
I DOUBT IT, DOUBT, SKEPTICAL: Place the right *V* hand before the eyes and bend and unbend the fingers a few times.
IS: Place the right *I* hand at

the mouth and move it forward.
LAWYER, ATTORNEY: Place the right *L* hand on the vertical left flat fingers and move the right *L* hand down to the left palm. End with the *person-ending* sign.
MACHINE, ENGINE, FACTORY, MOTOR: Place open hands in front of the body, palms in, and interlace the fingers. Move the hands up and down a few times at the wrists.

OFFER, PRESENT: With palms up, move the flat hands up and forward.
REJECT: Slide the right flat hand (bottom edge) over and past the left flat hand, palm up.
THE (definite article): Twist the right *T* hand to the right from a palm-left position.

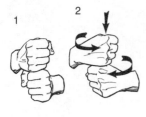    

fixed.   The   business   went

   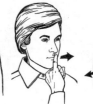

bankrupt.   He   is   a

famous   American   (individual).

A: Move the right *A* hand in a small arc to the right.
AMERICAN, AMERICA: Interlock the slightly curved open hands. Move them in a circle from right to left. Add the *person-ending* sign when using *American* in reference to a person.
BANKRUPT, BROKE: Hit the neck with the right bent hand.
BUSINESS: Tap the right *B-*hand wrist on the palm-down left closed-hand wrist

several times. Face the *B* hand forward.
INDIVIDUAL: Move both *I* hands down in unison in front of the chest, palms facing.
FAMOUS, FAME: Place both index fingers at the mouth and roll them out and up in small spirals.
FIX, MAKE: Hit the left *S* hand with the right *S* hand. Twist the hands in. Then repeat.
HE, HIM: Pretend to be

gripping a cap with the right hand. Move it forward a little. Then point the right index finger forward. If the gender is obvious, omit gripping a cap (the *male* sign).
IS: Place the right *I* hand at the mouth and move it forward.
THE (definite article): Twist the right *T* hand to the right from a palm-left position.
WENT: Rotate the index fingers around each other as they move forward.

The president spoke. Pay

  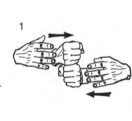 

the tax. I agree

(disagree). Who won

AGREE: Bring the right index finger to the forehead. Place both index fingers together, palms down, and other fingers closed in front of the chest.
DISAGREE, CONTRADICT: Place the right index finger on forehead. Touch the fingertips of both *D* hands and move them apart quickly.
I: Place the right *I* hand on the chest, palm left.
PAY: Place the right index finger in the left flat palm

and move the right index finger forward.
PRESIDENT: Place the *C* hands at the temples, palm forward. Move them up a little to the sides, ending in *S* hands.
SPOKE, SAY, SPEAK, SPEECH, TELL: Move the right index finger in a forward circle from the mouth.
TAX, COST, CHARGE, FINE, PRICE: Hit the right bent index finger across and down the left palm.

THE (definite article): Twist the right *T* hand to the right from a palm-left position.
WHO, WHOM: With the right index finger, make a circle in front of the lips.
WON, WIN: Bring open hands together, forming *S* hands, one over the other. Then make small circles with the raised right index fingertip and thumb tip touching.

the   election?   They   need

 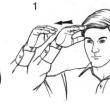 

our   support.   He

is   innocent   (guilty)   (foolish).

ELECTION, VOTE, ELECT: Move the right *F*-hand thumb and index finger down into the left *O* hand.

FOOLISH: With palm left, move the right *Y* hand back and forth in front of the forehead several times.

GUILTY: Tap the side of the right *G* hand on the heart area several times.

HE, HIM: Pretend to be gripping a cap with the right hand. Move it forward a little. Then point the right index finger forward. If the gender is obvious, omit gripping a cap (the *male* sign).

INNOCENT: Touch the mouth with both *H*-hand fingers and bring the hands down to the front, palms up.

IS: Place the right *I* hand at the mouth and move it forward.

NEED, HAVE TO, MUST, NECESSARY, SHOULD: Move the right bent index finger down forcefully several times.

OUR: Move the slightly cupped right hand in a semicircle from the right side to the left side of the chest.

SUPPORT: Push the right *S* hand up under the left *S* hand, moving both hands up a little

THEY, THEM, THESE, THOSE: Point forward or to the people or objects with the right index finger and move the hand to the right.

 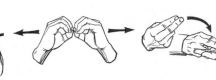

We · have · none. · Sign
signature

 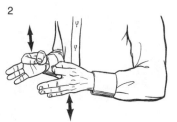

this. · The · judge

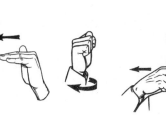 

was · fair. · The · thief

FAIR, EQUAL: Move both bent-hands fingertips together in front of the body several times.
HAVE, HAD, HAS, OWN, POSSESS: Move the bent-hands fingertips to chest.
JUDGE, COURT, JUDGE-MENT, JUSTICE, TRIAL: Place the right index finger on the forehead. Move the two *F* hands, palms facing, alternately up and down.
NONE: Place the *O* hands to the front with fingers

touching. Move them apart in opposite directions.
SIGN, SIGNATURE: Move the upturned right *H* fingers into the flat left palm.
THE (definite article): Twist the right *T* hand to the right from a palm-left position.
THIEF, BURGLAR, CROOK: Move the *H* hands apart from under the nose.
THIS: Place the right index finger in the left flat palm for something specific.
WAS: Move the right *W*

hand backward near the right cheek and close it to an *S* hand.
WE, US: Touch the right shoulder with the right index finger. Then, circle it forward and back until it touches the left shoulder. The *W* hand can be used for *we* and *U* hand for *us*.

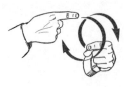  

went   to   prison.   My

  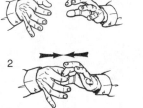

nephew   (niece)   joined   the

military.   Did   you

MILITARY, ARMY: Hold the right *A* hand near the left shoulder and the left *A* hand a little below it. Place the *C* hands in front, palms facing, and move them in a forward circle until the little fingers touch.

DID, ACTION, DO, DONE: Move both *C* hands, palms down, in unison to the left, then to the right.

JOIN, UNITE: Connect the thumbs and index fingers of both hands like the links of a chain. Keep other fingers extended.

MY, MINE, OWN: Place the right flat hand on the chest.

NEPHEW: Shake the right extended *N*-hand fingers near the right side of the head.

NIECE: Shake the right extended *N*-hand fingers back and forth near the right chin.

PRISON: Cross the open (or *B*)-hand fingers, palms in.

THE (definite article): Twist the right *T* hand to the right from a palm-left position.

TO: Touch the left vertical index fingertip with the right index fingertip.

WENT, GO: Rotate the index fingers around each other as they move forward.

YOU: Point to the person you are signing to. Move the right hand from left to right if there is more than one person.

vote?   I   am   a   Democrat

(Republican). It   is   a   law

(crime)   (government regulation).

....

A: Move the right *A* hand in a small arc to the right.
AM: Move the right *A*-hand thumb forward from the lips.
DEMOCRAT: Shake the right *D* hand with palm forward.
CRIME: Sign *bad* by touching the lips with the fingertips of the right flat hand. Then turn the hand and move it down with the palm facing down. Next, sign *sin* by holding both index fingers pointing at each other and

make simultaneous circles.
GOVERNMENT: Circle the right index finger at the temple, then touch the temple.
I: Place the right *I* hand on the chest, palm left.
IS: Place the right *I* hand at the mouth and move it forward.
IT: Touch the right *I* finger in the flat left palm.
LAW: Place the right *L* hand on the vertical left flat fingers and move the *L* hand down to the palm.

REGULATION: Place the right *R* hand on the vertical left flat fingers and move the *R* hand down to the left palm.
REPUBLICAN: Shake the right *R* hand with palm forward.
VOTE, ELECT, ELECTION: Move the right *F*-hand thumb and index finger down into the left *O* hand.

Do   you   have   [a]

degree?   plan?   question?   car?

Use any of the following signs.

will?   license?   job   experience?

CAR, DRIVE: Make two *S* hands. Pretend to be steering a car.

DEGREE, DIPLOMA: Hold the *O* hands to the front, palms down, and move them apart to the sides at the same time.

DO, DID, ACTION, DONE: *(See page 248.)*

EXPERIENCE: Touch the right temple with the right curved open hand and move it out a little, changing to an *and* hand.

HAVE, HAD, HAS, OWN, POSSESS: Move the bent-hands fingertips to the chest.

JOB, WORK: Tap the right *S*-hand wrist on the left *S*-hand wrist several times, palms down.

LICENSE, CERTIFICATE: Hold the *L* hands to the front, palms forward; tap the thumbs together several times. *Certificate* can be signed with *C* hands.

PLAN, ORDER: Hold both flat hands a little to the left, palms facing. Move them together to the right in small up-and-down movements.

QUESTION, QUESTION MARK: Draw a question mark in the air with the right index finger. Include the period.

WILL (legal statement): Place the right *W* hand on the vertical left flat fingers and move the *W* hand down to the left palm.

YOU: *(See page 248.)*

INDEX

The first usage of the sign is listed. Those in **bold** are main entry words. The light-face words are synonyms.